A GLIMPSE
OF HOW IT USED TO BE

I trust as you read this book,
you can reflect back to your own past
and memories and relate to these
incidences in this book.

Blessings,
Miriam Hochstetler
January 30, 2020

A GLIMPSE
OF HOW IT USED TO BE

Memories Of My Past Life

MIRIAM HOCHSTETLER

XULON PRESS

Xulon Press
2301 Lucien Way #415
Maitland, FL 32751
407.339.4217
www.xulonpress.com

Paperback ISBN-13: 978-1-6628-2423-4
Ebook ISBN-13: 978-1-6628-2424-1

DEDICATION

This book is dedicated to my wonderful parents, William and Mary Hochstetler, who provided Christian nurturing, modeled a strong work ethic, involved us in music appreciation, and maintained a loving stable home life for our family in predominantly a Mennonite and Amish rural community of Nappanee, Indiana.

William and Mary Hochstetler
Wedding Day – September 15, 1923

To My Interested Readers

May this book be an inspiration to you as I share with you many memories of my life in the family of my father, William Hochstetler, 1889-1959; my mother, Mary (Maust) Hochstetler, 1899-1996, and their children: Eugene Lewis, 1926-1932; Dean LaMar, 1928-2006; Mary Ellen, 1932-___; Miriam Elaine, 1934-___; and Alan Ray, 1939-2018.

1947 FAMILY PHOTO

Front row left to right: Miriam Hochstetler, age 13;
Alan Hochstetler, age 8; Mary Ellen Hochstetler, age 15
Back row left to right: Dean Hochstetler, age 19;
Mary Hochstetler (mother), age 48; William Hochstetler (father), age 58

TABLE OF CONTENTS

Chapter 1
A Metaphoric View Of Family Life

How many times have we said, "This was not in my plans! Why did this happen?" Without a doubt, life brings about imminent challenges, adjustments, and continual changes that may be difficult to accept. Critical issues pervade our society and the "family" can be a genuine target. It has been said that the family is the "glue" to the nation. Is it strong enough to withstand and counteract its adversaries?

One of the best ways to depict family life in general is with applicable metaphors. There are many to choose from and the following ten have been selected.

METAPHOR 1 – A JIG SAW PUZZLE
All the pieces of a jig saw puzzle must fit together correctly to complete the whole picture. The pieces can represent both parents and children working together and cooperating to provide a harmonious well-functioning family unit. My father tried to shove and push a few pieces of a puzzle into inappropriate spots and wondered why they didn't fit. This incident might represent a person in the family who has more difficulty functioning as part of the family. Help and guidance is needed in both situations.

METAPHOR 2 – FLOWERS IN A GARDEN

As flowers grow in a garden, each one has distinctive characteristics or features adding beauty and harmony. Quality care is required for optimum growth and blossoming. Members in any family also have their unique personalities, characteristics, and abilities that contribute to valuable integrated family interactions. They, too, need constant quality care, love, and attention to "bloom and blossom" into beautiful persons as God created them.

METAPHOR 3 – AN ELEVATOR

Elevators go up and down depending what button is pressed. They cannot stay in one position or neutral to accommodate people. A family has its "ups and downs" as each member reacts and interacts with the expected and unexpected circumstances. Sometimes it may feel like the "buttons" have been pushed too fast and too hard which can cause physical, psychological, and spiritual pressures that are often difficult to resolve. Staying neutral is not a win-win situation.

METAPHOR 4 – MOTOR VEHICLES

Motor vehicles have many parts that can break down and need repair to function properly. All a vehicle may require is a recharged battery. Nevertheless, proper maintenance may help to prevent malfunctioning parts. Family members sometimes have relational "break-downs" that also need to be recharged with "positive repairs" in face-to-face discussions so that meaningful and functional interactions can resume again. A spirit of forgiveness is an added gift available from God.

METAPHOR 5 – CONSTRUCTON OF A BUILDING

The construction of a building must first be built with a firm foundation so that the additional sections maintain support and stability. A family also requires a firm foundation by believing, utilizing, and applying biblical principles and morals that God has given us. Otherwise, instability and fractures can affect family lives during "stormy weather" episodes that may collapse.

METAPHOR 6 – A DEPENDABLE COMPASS

A dependable compass always points North. Our internal compass must always point to God as we endeavor to make the right and best choices with His guidance. His GPS is always accurate and dependable!

METAPHOR 7 – A GLASS HALF FULL OR HALF EMPTY

An attitudinal perspective may address this question: Is the drinking glass half empty or half full? Psychologically, the half full glass depicts a more positive position of life than the half empty one. In essence, viewing the family as a glass half full creates more positive, productive, and happier lives for everyone even though sometimes it seems easier to find the negative.

METAPHOR 8 – HIGHWAYS

Roads may be straight, hilly, and winding with lots of curves. There may be potholes, detours, and dead ends that necessitate driving adjustments in speed and direction. So, too, a family will meet obstacles along the way with "bumps and detours." The "pothole" moments of adversity and difficulty can test a family's unity in the approaches that are taken to resolve the issues. Whether they be temporary or permanent, can the road become "straight and smooth" again? What will make the difference?

METAPHOR 9 – TECHNOLOGICAL GADGETRY

Mobile phones, computers, Android smart phones, cell phones, iPhones, tablets, e-readers, Bluetooth speakers, laptops, fax machines, television, and many other current kinds of technological tools are available and easily accessible. As valuable and useful as they are for us, they can bring both undesirable and desirable messages and information. Do they control us or do we control them? Pressing the "delete" or "off" button can be done quickly to remove the undesirable. As we reflect on our lives and society at large, there are those things that require deletions so that we can live more abundantly, respectfully, and enjoyably. Here we need much discernment, discipline, and prayer so that we control the use of the contrivances that are so readily accessible. Observations can tell stories. Wherever you go, people seem consumed with their gadgets: at the airport, the doctor's office, in restaurants, shopping in stores, and while driving their cars. Families can be devoid of good conversations especially in restaurants when they are busily engaged in their hand-held tools. Our gadgets should never replace or be a substitute for intercommunications with our families and friends. Years past this was not an issue. So, do our lives become less personal as more current technology becomes available?

METAPHOR 10 – BEAUTIFUL TAPESTRIES

Beautiful tapestries can be made or purchased with various designs and words. Each of the dark and light-colored threads is woven, knitted, or stitched to create a particular pattern. It is as though they intersect and interact with each other. Each family member blends in with unique characteristics, personalities, skills, and abilities. Our tapestry of life blends in with our early days, traditions, culture, social interactions, values, and philosophy of life. They are all interwoven as they become our threads, the "fabric of life," as we live and interact with each other.

A quote from the book *God's Mysterious Ways* by Gary Inrig, 2016 copyright, quotes: *"Even a superficial analysis makes it clear that fractured families practice fractured lives. Those, in turn, lead to fractured communities, producing a downward spiral that will be ultimately reversed only if and when, in grace, intervenes."*

Does life seem more stressful, busier, and despondent even with all the current technological advances and conveniences that should make life easier and simpler? Another appropriate quote from *God's Mysterious Ways* sums it up well: *"We don't get to choose the times we live in, but we do get to choose how we live in those times."* All our gadgetry can take away crucial time that should be spent interacting with our children and families. So as we have "delete" buttons on our technological devices, we can also press the "delete" activities button that might interfere with premium quality of family life. Put on "save" and make "contact" with those activities that should be in our "high priority" list.

ENDING CHAPTER THOUGHTS

What does it take to build and maintain a family that has a firm foundation? On a more personal perspective, the following chapters will focus primarily on my PAST life including my parents and my siblings. Without growing up with many of the amenities that are considered necessities today, our family maintained a stable, cooperative and very functional life even with a strict adherence to biblical admonitions, a strong pervasive work ethic, and responsibilities. They were taken seriously for which I am truly thankful.

The next chapter will focus on "Major Building Blocks for a Firm Family Foundation" that involves the Hochstetler family as I reflect on my past and cherish the wonderful memories that have affected all of us throughout our adult lives.

The additional chapters will delineate specific portions of my life. My hope is that your life will be enriched as you travel down "memory lane" with me on my early journey beginning in 1934.

"THE FAMILY THAT PRAYS TOGETHER STAYS TOGETHER."

Chapter 2

MAJOR BUILDING BLOCKS FOR A FIRM FAMILY FOUNDATION

What keeps a family intact and functioning well? One of the most important factors is to consider the background of the parents. They are the family leaders and models that influence and impact us especially in the early formative years and extend into our adult lives. In addition, we need to recognize and realize the seriousness that our ancestors also played a major and crucial role in our lives. *In reference to Exodus 20:5, God says, "...I, the Lord your God, am a jealous God, punishing the children for the sin of their fathers to the third and fourth generations of those who hate me, but showing love to thousands who love me and keep my commandments."*

My father was born in 1899. To get a glimpse of his early background during the draft era and his belief system, he kept himself from the draft with a farm deferment as long as he could during World War I. Eventually, he was drafted and was located at Camp Taylor in Louisville, Kentucky. As a conscientious objector, the government had made no special provisions or exceptions. He had to remain steadfast in his convictions as he refused or defied the order to wear a uniform. Somehow, he was given the opportunity to serve in kitchen duty at the end of the War in 1918. In addition, he lived in a rural farming area and attended a one-room country schoolhouse for only several months out of the year to help with farming responsibilities. He had a Christian upbringing as well.

My mother was born in 1899. She also lived in a rural farming area and spoke about rising early in the morning around 4:00 to milk cows by hand before walking to school for a mile and a half. She obtained seven years of education as she had skipped first grade. She was a proficient student and could read before going to school. It was apparent she had a background of strict Christian fundamentals that her parents required of her as she was growing up.

In essence, what my parents both had in common were a number of factors: lived during World War I (1914-1918), World War II (1939-1945), and the Great Depression (1929-1939); came from Christian homes; lived a simple rural life; believed in frugality; chose friends carefully; guarded their finances; stayed out of debt; dressed in modest attire; had respect for others; and took a non-military stance. They were both hard-working disciplined persons. Living a frivolous life was not even in the picture.

Given this parental background, we grew up with our biological parents, not surrogates or other "family" systems and arrangements that our current society considers "marriage or family." Since they were both strong adherents of the Christian faith and lived by fundamental Christian biblical principles, those standards and guidelines were imparted to us. We saw it in action. Their values permeated every aspect of their lives and had an effect on us as well. The internal and external basic life systems and values, no doubt, were the building blocks of our firm family foundation well rooted and grounded with the following eight "Building Blocks" described below.

BUILDING BLOCK 1 – BIBLICAL AND SPIRITUAL TRUTHS

Referring to the biblical reference in I Corinthians 16:13, it admonishes people to stand firm in the faith: *"Be on your guard, stand firm in the faith, be of good courage, be strong. Do everything in love."* Another admonition to build a firm foundation is a command in Proverbs 22:6: *"Train up a child in the way he should go, and when he is old, he will not depart from it."* My parents were "models" of these attributes.

BUILDING BLOCK 2 – EATING MEALS TOGETHER

Eating meals together with everyone present was essential. Mother read a daily passage of scripture taken from the *Sunday School Quarterly*. Father then followed by prayer. Eating meals together created family time to eat and have conversations that contributed to the cohesiveness of a strong family. Our conversations were spoken in Pennsylvania Dutch, our dominant or primary language spoken at home, although we were bilingual before attending public school.

BUILDING BLOCK 3 – ATTENDING CHURCH SERVICES

Attending church services several times a week at North Main Street Mennonite Church, Nappanee, Indiana, was not optional in our family. I don't ever remember being reluctant to attend church. It was such a usual or normal thing to do without questioning or provocation. We attended Sunday morning and evening services every week faithfully. Sunday School classes were available and friends in the class were part of our support group. A *Sunday School Quarterly* contained weekly Bible lessons that were to be read at home and discussed later in class.

BUILDING BLOCK 4 – THE FAMILY WORK ETHIC

Our parents were arduous workers and completed their tasks with neatness and precision. Father was a carpenter and always had jobs in the community and more distant places that necessitated traveling in his Model T Ford. There were jobs to do at home such as filing saws for others, spading a large garden, spraying many fruit trees, explaining blueprints of projected buildings that people were aspiring to build, and tending the honey bees. Mother tended the vegetable garden, canned and froze fruit, sewed our homemade clothes, and cooked nutritious meals daily.

We were given daily routine responsibilities that varied according to need and seasonal requirements. We were expected to help in any way that was necessary without complaining. The job that was started was to be completed. We were given no allowance and I am not sure why. We also found out that an admonition should not be repeated. Being told once was sufficient and we obeyed. I don't ever remember being yelled at for any reason. It just did not happen even though there was "discipline" enacted in our home. We knew our parents appreciated our help, cared for us, and loved us even though we never heard the three words verbally, "I love you!" Today I am thankful that I do enjoy working and attempt to finish what I have begun.

BUILDIING BLOCK 5 – FAMILY SINGING TIME

We were fortunate to have a father who was very musical and made a special effort to have us sing hymns with him in four- part harmony (soprano, alto, tenor, bass). Initially, we had a pump organ and later an upright piano which I began to play at a young age. We learned to read notes, regard proper timing, and enjoy singing unfamiliar hymns with each of us singing our designated part while I accompanied us on the piano. One Sunday evening we sang only unfamiliar hymns from a book we had just purchased. We sang for several hours. What a wonderful use of time to sing when we had no television and radio. Singing together was one of the most memorable and treasurable times. Today my sister and I like to sing. I play the organ and we enjoy listening to choral and orchestral music.

BUILDING BLOCK 6 – FAMILY TRIPS

Family trips were infrequent but when they were taken, they were quite significant and special. One early morning while the neighbor's rooster was crowing, we prepared for a trip to the Brookfield Zoo and the Science and Industry Museum in Chicago. Since our Father believed that driving only thirty miles per hour was fast enough in our 1936 Chevrolet on busy streets and highways, we finally arrived safely to these destinations without a problem or a warning ticket of driving too slowly!

One major family trip took us to Puerto Rico in 1952 to visit our older brother, Dean, who was serving two years in 1-W Service under the auspices of Mennonite Central Committee to satisfy draft requirements for conscientious objectors. A train took us near Kennedy Airport or formerly named Idlewild Airport. Our Eastern Airline flight was on a non-jet plane that took us through a frightening thunder storm. We were very thankful to arrive safely. Visiting in a different culture with Spanish speaking people was an unforgettable experience. Another memorable occasion was viewing deep sea life in a glass-bottomed boat ride in the Atlantic Ocean. It was absolutely fascinating!

A quick excursion took us to Henry Ford Museum in Michigan and also to Niagara Falls. Nine of us were "packed" in a station wagon enjoying every moment of those trips.   Another very long trip for all of us was traveling to San Francisco, California, to meet my brother, Alan, who had served for three years in Vietnam and Korea during draft time in PAX (peace) service with Mennonite Central Committee. It was a happy reunion except for the fact that our Father had died during the time Alan was gone. One of the most joyous and exhilarating experiences was singing "How Great Thou Art" while driving through the Rocky Mountains. It was breath-taking and awesome!

BUILDING BLOCK 7 – ALWAYS BE HONEST

Our Mother was a "moral code" builder. Honesty was expected from us in all situations. She mentioned that when she was growing up, a verbal answer or a handshake was sufficient to show the other person that you can be trusted. She also told us that if we made a mistake or did something wrong, we should always tell the truth and there would be no punishment. That is exactly what happened! Fear was not a factor and neither was punishment! I never forgot that nugget of truth and advice. I applied it later on in my own classroom with elementary students. She recited a short poem and I quote:

> *"Speak the truth and speak it ever*
> *Cost it what it will;*
> *He who hides the wrong he did*
> *Does the wrong thing still."*

BUILDING BLOCK 8 – LIVE FRUGALLY

Live frugally, simply, and practically. Spend your money wisely. Use what you have or is available until it does not work or cannot be repaired. We did not know what it was like to live extravagantly. There were no credit cards or debit cards available and lay-away options were not even considered. You paid in cash. We were not poor or rich and did not require the latest or most modern style of anything. I remember my Mother saying, "Why do things have to match?" Color schemes were not important to her. We lived comfortably, worked hard, and were basically happy. It has been said, *"If you can't afford it, don't buy it. It's not how much you have but how you use what you have."*

TWO APPLICABLE SONGS

A hymn, "How Firm a Foundation," verse two, is very appropriate and comforting:

"Fear not! I am with thee, O be not dismayed,
For I am thy God and will still give thee aid.
I'll strengthen thee, help thee, and cause thee to stand,
Upheld by my righteous, omnipotent hand."

A familiar picturesque children's song usually sung with motions can be an analogy to a family and the type of "building blocks" it pursues. (The repetition of words has been omitted). Quote:

"A foolish man built his house upon the sand,
And the rains came tumbling down.
The rains came down and the floods came up,
And the house on the sand went ___ (clap only).

The wise man built his house upon the rock,
And the rains came tumbling down
The rains came down and the floods came up
And the house on the rock stood firm."

CONCLUDING COMMENTS

These positive and essential "building blocks" we experienced did contribute to a functional family life impacting our adult lives. A few nuggets of encouragement may be helpful: persevere through difficult situations; enjoy the pleasantries of life fully; change what can be changed and accept that which cannot be changed – be discerning of the difference; adjust as best as is possible to a constant changing society; and pray for wisdom and discernment when making decisions. *Life may be compared to tapestry when all the "threads" of life are woven together in a manner to provide and enhance a productive and happy outcome.*

It is imperative we take time for each other as families and grasp the opportunities to accomplish and maintain a solid foundation lest it may gradually crumble! Time has a way of getting away from us quickly.

Chapter 3

CHURCH ATTENDANCE, PRACTICES, AND DOCTRINE

IMPORTANCE OF HONORING THE SABBATH

I s Sunday a day to "sleep in" or a "catch up" on our agenda with unfinished work that was not accomplished during the week? There must be a good reason why God commanded a day of rest each week for us. Just what does this day of rest do for our minds and bodies? If God rested on the Sabbath day, what are the implications for us?

A few scripture verses speak about the holiness of that day:

Genesis 2:2-3 says: "By the seventh day God had finished the work he had been doing; so, on the seventh day he rested from all his work. And God blessed the seventh day and made it holy, because on it he rested."

Exodus 16:23 speaks about God instructing Moses to give the Israelites this message: "This is what the Lord commanded. Tomorrow is to be a day of rest, a holy Sabbath to the Lord."

Exodus 20:8-11 and Deuteronomy 5:12-15 both remind us to regard the Sabbath: "Observe or remember the Sabbath by keeping it holy. Six days you shall labor and do all your work, but the seventh day is a Sabbath to the Lord your God. On it you shall not do any work."

Exodus 31:14 provides this command: "Observe the Sabbath, because it is holy to you. For six days work is to be done but the seventh day is a Sabbath of rest, holy to the Lord."

Some children may ask their parents, "Are we going to church today?" Others may be taken to church but their parents do not attend the services. What kind of testimony and modeling are they exhibiting to their children? My parents considered church attendance a priority and no questions were ever necessary. Today it has become very convenient listening to church services using technological services such as Zoom, You Tube, and Live Streaming on the computer or other devices and stay comfortable in our own homes.

In retrospect, Sunday was a day of rest or a change for us from weekday responsibilities at work. It was also a reprieve from teaching students for me. Sunday morning breakfast consisted of a brief devotional time, dipping our bread slices with homemade apple butter into a cup of hot cocoa, and drinking the rest of it. Then it was time to get "ready" for church.

A man who lived about a mile from us walked down his lane to the main road every Sunday morning to go to church with us. As he sat in the front seat of the car beside me, I noticed he was sucking on something that smelled like prunes. From then on, we referred to him as the "prune man" and finally realized that the "prune" smell was actually from a cough drop. As we continued the four miles to North Main Street Mennonite Church, Nappanee, Indiana, there was always OUR spot to park by Wilbur Lehman's apple tree and people seemed to respect that. There was no parking or reserve sign with William Hochstetler's name inscribed on it. I don't ever remember someone taking our special spot.

INTERIOR CHURCH STRUCTURE
The exterior brick structure of the church showed simplicity as did the interior. There were no ornate motifs inside – just plain windows,

benches in the sanctuary and balcony, and the congregants were divided: men sat on the south side and the women on the north side of the sanctuary facing the pulpit during the church service. I do not know the reason other than it was tradition. There were two "Amen" corners with a few benches for the elderly. Historically, there were various denominations other than Mennonite churches that had "Amen" corners. Again, the men sat on the south side and the women on the north side. I do not recall anyone yelling out "AMEN" any time during the service confirming or expressing assent to a statement the preacher might have made or a response to a prayer request. I got permission to sit with my grandmother in the "Amen" corner one Sunday morning and I considered it a special treat.

DESCRIPTION OF CHURCH SERVICES

The man preaching in the pulpit was our "preacher," the terminology used rather than "pastor." It was considered wrong and unheard of to have Mennonite women pastor a church during this time. A minister was usually not paid a salary for his ongoing work of the church. Therefore, it necessitated finding an additional job to support himself. Fortunately, that finally changed when churches supported their minister full time with additional amenities. Air conditioning was not available, but with open windows and hand-held fans provided by a funeral home or having your own helped to keep the air flowing somewhat. Children were expected to behave during an adult service while often squirming and sitting so long on a hard bench. Parents often provided "quiet" toys and books to keep their children occupied. There was no children's church. Parents with babies were also in the audience and if the baby cried, usually the mother took the child out of the sanctuary. I have often wondered how children were expected to "survive" an adult church service with short attention spans and how satisfactory the parents could worship and enjoy the services. Finally, a child nursery became available, crying babies could be removed from the audience, and the congregants worship undisturbed.

There were no musical instruments in the church to provide an introduction or beginning tone of any hymn. So, the chorister or song leader had a circular shaped pitch pipe with all the notes including sharps and flats engraved on the outer edges. After the chorister determined the key of the song, he blew into that space on the pitch pipe which produced the correct tone necessary to begin that particular hymn. When my father was church chorister, he used a tuning fork in a certain key and hit it gently on the hymnbook so he could determine what pitch to begin the first note of the hymn. We still have that special tuning fork. Whatever method was used, Mennonites were known for their beautiful four-part acapella singing which continues today. There were occasional hymn-sings on Sunday evenings when a number of local Mennonite churches would get together and sing some of their favorite hymns. In addition, there was special music. A quartet might sing several selections. It was an enjoyable time of worship and to socialize with many friends after the service.

Praying was a very important part of the church service. We often knelt on our knees facing the back of the bench rather than standing or just bowing our heads while sitting. Several of my friends and I were not always reverent during prayer. We would each have a hymnbook as we knelt and had a competitive race as to which person would be the first to find a specified page. We also whispered at times and giggled "quietly." Why we did this I do not know, but I knew this was inappropriate behavior!

A man by the name of Mitchell memorized many scripture verses with their references. Occasionally, on a Sunday morning, he would stand in front of the congregation, clasp his hands in front of him, and with a robust and powerful voice recite those verses with delight. One could tell they meant a lot to him. His ability to memorize was mesmerizing and awesome. What a challenge and inspiration he left for all of us!

BIBLICAL DOCTRINES UPHELD BY THE MENNONITE CHURCH

We brought our Bibles to church so that scripture passages read by the preacher or moderator could be followed. I do not recall any specific sermon but I do remember a few biblical "commands" based on the interpretations of certain scripture passages. We were to refrain from following "worldly" practices that were considered sinful or not biblical: do not attend movies or theaters; do not wear lip stick, slacks, shorts, or jewelry; do not swear or take an oath; and do not dance or drink alcoholic beverages. Once I sniffed into an empty beer can that was found along the road. That one sniff made me wonder how any person could drink the "smelly" stuff.

Of major importance was another command that women should not cut their hair based on 1 Corinthians 11:14-15 that states: *"Does not the very nature of things teach you that if a man has long hair, it is a disgrace to him, but that if a woman has long hair, it is her glory? For long hair is given to her as a covering."* Young girls often had braided hair with long "pigtails" as they were called hanging down their back.

Another very important church doctrine was women wearing a head "covering" during church services based on *I Corinthians 11:3-5: "...the head of every man is Christ, and the head of the woman is man, and the head of Christ is God. Every man who prays or prophesies with his head covered dishonors his head. And every woman who prays prophesies with her head uncovered dishonors her head – it is just as though her head were shaved."* Mother strictly required and expected us to wear our covering at meals since we had prayer before eating. She made her own head covering and wore it all the time. She made her own simple styled "bonnets" and wore them when she left home.

OTHER CHURCH RELATED OPPORTUNITIES

Sunday School classes for all ages were available as everyone was grouped according to age ranges. As we got older, we had specific lessons to read each Sunday from our quarterlies published by the Mennonite Publishing House. We were encouraged to read them at home first so that the topics could be discussed well during the Sunday School class.

Sunday evening services consisted of several people speaking on topics they prepared and presented to the congregation. Mother helped me write my first topic. On my assigned Sunday evening, I walked nervously up to the pulpit and read my essay. I was very glad when I was finished. Later on, I wrote my own ideas for assigned topics.

Bible School classes were usually held for one or two weeks during the summer months on weekday evenings. We were given recitations or Bible verses to memorize for a program. I remember standing in fear waiting for my turn. That fear was forgetting some of the lines or going "blank" altogether. There was always an adult assistant nearby should one need help. What a relief it was when my part was finished! I do believe that the early teaching experiences with elementary aged children in Bible School classes, Sunday School classes, and singing with them each Sunday morning helped me to become a certified or licensed elementary school teacher. Teaching in my own classroom, eventually assisting other classroom teachers, and later teaching students in college who were interested in becoming elementary school teachers were golden opportunities to serve others in education.

North Main Street Mennonite Church became a large congregation with over 400 people who attended. Chairs were placed in the aisles to accommodate those who came too late to sit on the benches in the sanctuary or balcony. A part of the mission output was to help with a church in Osceola, Indiana, where I taught a class for some time. Much later in my adult years, another Mennonite Church began in Bourbon, Indiana. Most of the people who attended there came from North Main Street Mennonite Church on a voluntary basis. Homer North was our preacher at the time of this expansion and increase in attendance. The youth group was named MYF (Mennonite Youth Fellowship) and had a membership of at least 100 people. We were involved in mission projects planting potatoes, tomatoes, and popcorn and all the proceeds would be donated to charity.

Each year in the fall, evangelistic meetings occurred toward the end of one week for several evenings. A visiting or guest preacher was invited to speak. At each meeting, an open invitation was given to accept Jesus as our Savior and told how important it was to do that. People were highly encouraged to attend.

A special older man in our church named Anthony always treated the younger children with NECCO candy. Each piece was hard and circular with different colors or flavors available. We would run quickly to him after church and wait until he pulled the candy out of his pocket. I preferred the brown and the black licorice flavors and hoped there were always some left for me.

Lots of visiting occurred after our church service ended on a Sunday morning. It was not unusual to be invited to a home for the noon meal. These invitations usually came unexpectedly. Sometimes several families were invited and the fellowship was wonderful as well as the food.

Today we seldom gather in someone's home for a meal but, instead, drive to a restaurant or drive-in. Why is this happening?

Sometimes teenagers invited their friends to join them in their home after Sunday morning church services to eat and play games. On some Sunday evenings, the youth had fun times together. This was also an opportunity for dates to occur.

Church business meetings were usually held once a month after the service ended and an enticing potluck meal was then served! The temptation to eat too much delicious home cooked food was always present. Visiting with others while seated around the circular tables was a pleasant experience.

When we were teenagers, we joined other adults and went Christmas caroling for various people in their homes. Sometimes we rode in the church bus or in separate cars. The group ended at the preacher's house for hot chocolate, cookies, and socialization.

My father was the church treasurer. I was fascinated at the amount of money he brought home to count, particularly, the piles of coins that were placed into special bank coin paper rolls with their identification printed on the outside.

A PERSONAL EMBARRASSING STOCKING EXPERIENCE

As I relate this personal story about a "stocking" episode one Sunday morning years ago, it still seems fresh in my mind. Mother had purchased some cotton stockings (we did not call them hosiery at that time) for me to wear to church. I thought the color was a bit too orange, and I did not want to wear them. It would be too embarrassing, I thought! However, my Mother insisted! I must have fussed and complained too much for my parents to endure any more of my whining and lamenting. The next thing that happened was a spanking in the kitchen from my Father who used a small water dipper to teach me a lesson. My mouth shut quickly and the unlikeable stockings were worn to church that morning. I was utterly embarrassed and hoped that no one would notice them. I do not recall if I had to wear them again. At our house, you did what you were told. We knew we should be obedient. I do not remember ever getting another spanking. It was certainly something to avoid.

SOMETHING TO REMEMBER

Remember this: Regardless of who we are, where we live, our church affiliation or denomination, God is still on the throne and in control of our lives no matter the circumstances. He continues to love us in spite of our upbringing, the mistakes we have made, and church differences. We need to be sure we are bound for our heavenly home, the Celestial City! A lot of changes and adjustments have been made in construction of church buildings, doctrines, and society at large throughout our years but one thing is certain: GOD HAS NOT CHANGED AND WILL NOT CHANGE.

Chapter 4

MEMORABLE FAMILY TIMES

D o you ever hear someone say, "We never seem to have time to get together as a family? Does "time" regulate our lives or do we regulate time? One must regard family time as a high priority or else something else will easily and quickly replace it. Our family time included a variety of activities and events mentioned below.

AT THE TABLE

We had routine meals sitting at the same designated spot at the table. Breakfast was also devotional time with Mother reading scripture followed with prayer by my Father. There were conversations on various topics. When my Father spoke firmly, he would sometimes lift and shake his fork indicating that this was a serious issue.

SINGING TOGETHER

Singing together at home around the piano was one of the most unforgettable and treasurable memories. Our musical Father played the guitar and violin. He obtained an organ correspondence certificate of 50 lessons, provided singing classes for those who were interested in learning the fundamentals of music, and enjoyed attending local choral and instrumental concerts.

We bought a hymnbook at the local Christian Book Store and sang all the unfamiliar songs for several hours one evening until the book was finished. Without a doubt, this helped me to sight-read music and improve as I continued to play the piano – playing without professional lessons. I wrote the notes in pencil on the music page and on the piano keys. Beginning to play with one finger and ending by playing with both hands finally was a moment of great accomplishment for me. Sometimes my Father sat on the piano bench with me and clapped the timing or rhythm of the song. Unfortunately, proper fingering techniques are still a problem for me.

The musical experiences at home during my formative years had a great impact on my life from there on. Today I have my own church organ and play for several different churches. In the past I played for weddings and funerals. Weddings have changed considerably with couples making their own selections using other types of music they prefer. I have led a women's ensemble and a hand chime choir consisting of eleven players who played three octaves of music. These musical groups opened opportunities to provide programs in jails, nursing homes, assisted living arrangements, and churches.

I remember so well the time when my Father was sitting in a rocking chair leafing through a songbook selecting songs for his funeral when he spoke these encouraging words to me while I was sitting at the piano: "Don't ever forget your music." I promised him I would not forget. I believe he saw God-given musical talent while I was growing up and wanted me to continue that gift. Music is certainly my "spirit-lifter."

FAMILY GET-TOGETHERS

Mother's brother, Ralph, and his wife were guests for meals at our house. One could be assured that he would have a joke to tell or read one as he pulled a paper from his shirt pocket. The comical reading added a hearty laugh for all of us.

Celebrating family birthdays and holidays provided such fun times. Our nephews would enjoy hearing about my sister's nursing experiences and my teaching episodes. Sometimes other serious events were discussed. In the afternoon came game time that consisted of playing Aggravation, a board game with marbles, that holds "true" to its name! Probe, a word game, was always a challenge using alphabet letters to form words in connected ways on the game board. Mother often selected more difficult short-lettered words. Occasionally, she would say, "I have to go get my list!" In fact, this list remained a mystery until she died. Later on, we found it tucked neatly in a tablet by some dishes in the kitchen cabinet.

STROLLING THROUGH THE WOODS

We would take leisurely walks through a neighbor's woods with our Father on a Sunday afternoon. He would provide each of us with a sturdy twig or stick to be used as a cane while walking through the brush. Trees were identified and sometimes we sat on a log and listened to the chirping birds singing their happy songs. It was such a peaceful, quiet, and relaxing learning time. There was one scary moment as we continued to walk along the brush. Something on the ground resembled a glove! On further scrutiny, it was a coiled snake and its colors blended in with the soil and its surroundings. It did not stick out its tongue or move. Perhaps it was dead but whether dead or alive, we were thankful that it was not picked up for a glove!

ONE DAY EXCURSION AT THE BROOKFIELD ZOO

To expand our trip, driving to Chicago Brookfield Zoo in our 1936 Chevrolet amidst fast moving traffic, toll roads, and high-rise buildings was such a contrast with our rural area where we lived with cars, trucks, buggies, and horses with their clip-clopping hoofs pounding down on our roads. We never had to worry that Father would exceed any speed limits since he drove 30 miles per hour at the maximum. There were times when I wondered if we were in danger going too slowly among other faster-moving vehicles. Part of the day was spent at the Science and Industry Museum. Thankfully, we arrived there safely and returned home with a day of great enjoyment and satisfaction.

TWO -WEEK TRIP TO PUERTO RICO

Our two-week trip to Puerto Rico was our first unforgettable non-jet plane trip on Eastern Airlines to visit my brother, Dean, who was in IW service for two years. Our long train ride from Indiana took us to New York Idlewild (Kennedy) Airport. I observed a man having a lot of difficulty walking while the train was moving. He almost landed in my lap. At the time I wondered why he had so much trouble with his balance. Later on, I tried walking while the train was moving and I quickly understood why the man had problems.

While our flight continued to Puerto Rico, it became quite scary. The plane hit "air pockets" which are up and down vertical currents that cause a lot of turbulence. A storm was causing the rough flight that made our pillows fly up from our seats. Someone nearby was screaming and ripping a curtain off the window. There were more problems: Father could not hear; Mother needed oxygen; my brother vomited into a bag; and my sister and I were absolutely scared. The up and down motion was unsettling. Once we hit an air pocket and instantly the plane went down a good number of feet. By then I was sure we were skimming over the water in the Atlantic Ocean. Of course, with fastened seat belts, passengers were kept from flying out of their seats. Alas, the turbulence ended and we arrived safely in Puerto Rico.

During our visit there, we traveled on mountainous curvy roads and treacherous passes. It was an absolute necessity to drive cautiously to avoid hitting people and animals as they walked on the roads. In one instance, there were pigs in a house. Malnourished children were seen with bloated stomachs. On Sunday we attended a Spanish church. I remember my Father trying to sing Spanish from the hymn book during congregational singing. I found it quite amusing for I had several years of Spanish in high school and college and found it easier to read the words. Surprisingly, not only people were in church but some chickens walked in as well. I don't think they came to worship!

Some of the native foods were bananas that we ate so often until we lost an appetite for them. We also drove to a fast-food drive-in that was comparable or similar to our Dairy Queen in the USA and got a very large ice cream cone. While eating this one quickly, we were on our way to another Dairy Queen and "devoured" another cone. As one can surmise, the Hochstetlers do like and enjoy their ice cream!

When it was time to return to the USA, we were dreading our flight home because of our unpleasant plane trip to Puerto Rico. Fortunately, it was without weather related turbulence! Coming back to Indiana, we were most grateful for a safe trip and happy to be home.

LONG TRIP TO SAN FRANCISCO, CALIFORNIA

Our brother, Alan, left for Vietnam in 1958 for a three-year PAX (peace) term under the auspices of Mennonite Central Committee. He also served in Korea the last part of his term. During this time, our Father passed away, September 1959. When Alan's three-year term ended, our older brother, Dean, his wife, their four children, Mother, Mary Ellen, and I took a long trip in Dean's "station wagon" to San Francisco to meet Alan at the airport. (Those large vehicles were called station wagons, not vans in those days!) While sitting in the lounge at the airport waiting for his arrival, Alan appeared. After a three-year absence, it was so good to see him again. We felt jam-packed in the station wagon with him included on our way home – ten of us!

There were a few calamities that occurred on our trip. First, a wheel bearing broke on one of the wheels and time-out was needed to fix it. Also, some items in the packed trunk had to be removed to reach the tools. Second, a luggage bag with a zipper was attached securely to the top of the station wagon. After traveling a bit after leaving our motel, a person in a car flagged us and told us that our bag on top of the car was open. Apparently, it had not been closed properly. Upon checking the contents of the bag, two coats were missing – my Mother's coat and mine. We turned around and sped down the road looking for them alongside of the road but we never found them. Third, when we had stopped to visit a forest ranger area in a hilly setting, Verle, our very young nephew, fell and slid down a hill and could not stop until he got to a road. Fortunately, he escaped unhurt! Fourth, when traveling late at night in Nevada hoping to find a place to sleep, we drove and drove through sparse territory until we finally came to a lodging place that had only one room for all ten of us. We were packed like sardines in a container! Most of us slept on the floor and several were crowded in one bed. We stepped over and around each other to use the bathroom. Only two sets of towels were available so there was not much washing for any of us. I am not sure how much sleep occurred that night. It was now time to get up and move on since it was finally morning.

Driving through Death Valley on our way was a short-cut and vastly different but intriguing as there were water tanks beside the road or "path" available should the vehicle become overheated. It was very hot and sand dunes were the prominent landscape. The sparse desert-like vegetation was different. We drove with windows closed, air conditioning on, and drank a lot of water. There was a path that indicated where other cars had traveled. Perhaps they, too, took a short-cut from one destination to the other. Driving through Death Valley was a good learning experience but I certainly was glad to leave it too. Driving through there alone would be foolish in my opinion.

Just traveling far West brought in picturesque landscape. Various kinds of cacti, palm trees, and Joshua trees were prominent. Lee, our very youngest nephew, called the Joshua trees "Goshy trees." That brought a good laugh! Driving among the giant and stately Redwood trees was breath-taking. One tree was cut open wide and high enough for a car to drive through. We all wrapped and extended our arms around one tree as much as possible and still could not surround it completely. The trees were so tall that even while leaning backward and looking up, the tops of them could not be seen.

A very inspirational time was driving through the majestic Rocky Mountains. We sang "How Great Thou Art" and other great songs as God's marvelous creation in nature was manifested in so many ways. Certainly, we can say, "Our God is an awesome God!" The entire trip West to get Alan was worth every penny and every minute. It was good to get back in our rural area with horses and buggies and wonderful Indiana neighbors.

SHORT EXCURSION TO HENRY FORD MUSEUM AND NIAGARA FALLS

A short trip to the Henry Ford Museum, Greenwich Village, in Dearborn, Michigan, was a quick decision as we packed into Dean's station wagon again. After visiting there, we traveled to Niagara Falls which was absolutely awesome. Both trips were valuable as it was good to see another part of our great world in a different way.

PARTIAL FAMILY TRIP TO EUROPE

Mary Ellen, Alan, and I flew to Europe on Icelandic Airlines in 1969 and arrived in Luxembourg to get our leased car, a Volkswagen, that we had applied for allowing us to travel on our own for six weeks with maps and booklets that provided important information. We visited recommended places of interest in Germany, Switzerland, Holland,

and Austria. The Autobahn was a fast-moving super highway with no designated speed limits. Alan said he felt he had to drive more from his rearview mirror to cope with the fast traffic. Leasing a car gave us leisurely time to drive through the countryside to see people working in their fields and sometimes stopping to have conversations with them.

We visited a former German exchange student that was in my sister's high school graduating class. While in Germany, we visited a former second grade student of mine while teaching in Griffith, Indiana. It was good to make contact with a former Goshen College classmate, Janet Yoder, in Brussels, Belgium.

Germany was of special interest to us since our ancestors had lived there. We saw signs with letters "Hoch" as in Hochstadt 4km. a number of times. The Black Forest area was significant since we could relate better to those people both in language and culture. Their language or vernacular was similar to our Pennsylvania Dutch that we speak in the USA. They commented that it was like "Schwabish." Of special interest was the lattice work and flower boxes in windows. To find lodging one night, we stopped at a place that appeared as a motel or "place to sleep." Alan walked into the people's home and came back to our car grinning because this building was not for people but only for horses. We had a hearty good laugh! We also stayed in a German home where we watched on their television the first astronaut fly to the moon. The most gruesome and solemn place was in Dachau visiting a concentration building with a sign outside the entrance that stated, "NEVER AGAIN," in four different languages. Twisted metal body forms were also visible at the entrance representing dead bodies during the holocaust. As we entered the building, there were photographs of people who had suffered during Hitler's terrible reign killing millions of Jews. A huge pile of shoes was shown in a large photograph. A whipping bench with a whip was visible. Ashes could be seen in the incinerators. Visitors in the building spoke in soft low voices as it seemed eerily quiet. Later on, we visited Hitler's hide-out in another part of Germany.

We were shopping in a store in Austria and soon had a number of clerks wanting to help us. We were not really interested in buying anything in particular, so speaking in our Pennsylvania Dutch language we would reply, "Yousht gooka!" or "just looking!" They noticed our tennis shoes we were wearing and quickly identified us as Americans.

They were also excited that Americans could speak a language similar to theirs. We drove to a glacier and saw cracks in the ice and a warning sign to "travel at your own risk." Alan dared to take a stint over some of the glacier and we feared for his life should he make a mistake or the glacier start moving. We were relieved that he returned safely. We saw a monument of Martin Luther, a renowned early Christian leader. A boat ride on the Rhine River was very relaxing. We met a man and his wife who were German schoolteachers. They invited us to their home and also to visit their school. They provided us with a few German children's books. It was a delight to be with them.

Castles dotted the landscape in many places. Each one had its own unique features. One castle had such immaculate floors that we were asked to remove our shoes and wear slippers that were provided. Another castle had intricate wood carvings while another one had glass walls. It was difficult to stay in those rooms very long. Gold fixtures were prominent in one as well. There are stories of the kings and other relevant information about these different castles.

With more leisure time, we drove to the border of Hungary where there was a red and white fence, barbed wire, a watchtower, and possibly land mines. We went no further in that a couple who had stopped by told us that the people in the tower will shoot if necessary. It was not a good feeling–a feeling to leave now! We drove into the checkpoint in Czechoslovakia and decided this was not good for us either. We made an immediate turn-around and left.

In Switzerland, the roofs of some of the houses almost touched the ground. The fondue, a dip consisting of cheese, wine and seasonings, had different flavors. Yodelers gave us a unique opportunity to hear them in person.

Visiting a salt mine was an unusual experience. An elevator took us down to where we were put on rail cars to move around the mine a bit more.

Our trip to Europe provided opportunities for many first-time experiences. It was good to return after six weeks of traveling as we refueled in Iceland and on to the United States. We felt there was no better place to live!

THOUGHTS TO PONDER

1. What are the priorities for our families?
2. Does technology take the place of or interfere with memorable family times and celebrations?
3. What family activities can be achieved without major expenses?
4. What hold families together? Is it gadgetry or the human touch?

Chapter 5

EDUCATIONAL DAYS

D oes formal education guarantee a successful life? Can a person who has only an eighth-grade education be just as successful as a college graduate? Are the aptitudes, knowledge, and skills acquired through formal education adequate to meet the challenges in our ever-changing world? What other personal characteristics and qualifications are needed to be successful?

THE EDUCATION OF MY PARENTS

Glancing back to the past in the latter 1800's, both my parents had minimal formal education. My Father was born in 1889 and attended a one-room country school about three months out of a year until age twenty-one because he was needed on the farm. Even so, he became self-educated in several areas, especially mathematics, as he applied those skills for fifty years in his carpentry work drawing blueprints, constructing barns, houses, a feed mill, and discussing building plans with people. He also built special items: his own compartmentalized tool chest; wooden pedestals; chests to store quilts, comforters, and other materials; a wooden bed; a two-door cherry cupboard; bedroom closets; and two three-drawer wooden filing cabinets to store our college papers. He helped me with difficult eighth grade math story problems. For my college science class project, he made an eleven-scaled wooden xylophone in the key of C with graded lengths of wood for each note with an accompanying wooden mallet to strike the keys. He obviously functioned very well with a limited amount of formal education.

My Mother was born in 1899 and lived on the farm. She spoke about getting up at four o'clock in the morning to milk cows before walking about a mile and a half to a country school called Locke. She attended there for seven years, skipped first grade, and finished the eighth grade. She was a precocious child, could read before she went to school, and was academically at the top of her class. Poems were memorized while she was in school as she would recite them to us occasionally – a feat that may no longer occur in our schools today. It was amazing how many she remembered.

In 1978, she wrote an essay, "The Empty Nest," and presented it to our church audience one Sunday morning. At the age of 79, she wrote another essay, "A Grandmother's View of the Past," and presented it to my Early Childhood Education college class while I was teaching at Manchester College. Mother was an avid reader all her adult life, had an extensive vocabulary, and an outstanding memory!

OUR EARLY PUBLIC SCHOOL EDUCATIONAL YEARS

With this kind of brief educational background of my parents, our generation has experienced considerable educational differences. Two of my siblings began their first year or two at a country school named Muncie. We all attended a small-town public school in Bremen, Indiana, riding the school bus. Our bus was No. 9 driven by a very firm and excellent driver who used his rear-view mirror to "supervise" or "keep an eye" on any person that could cause a problem. We finally nicknamed him "Google Eye" and he carried out the description. Nevertheless, he transported us safely to and from school.

Mother woke us up each morning and we knew that calling us ONCE was often enough, especially on school mornings. More frequent calling on a given morning spelled trouble or dissatisfaction and we knew it. It was a discipline that required obedience and taking responsibility.

She packed our daily school lunches that varied from day to day in brown paper sacks and Alan's lunch in a blue dinner pail. Sandwiches consisted of peanut butter with raisins or pickles and occasionally meatloaf. Other food items were celery, carrot sticks, cookies, and whatever else was available. We never bought our lunch in the school cafeteria even though it was available. Mother certainly believed as long as we had our own food, it was not necessary to buy school lunches!

My hairless doll went with me on the bus occasionally. Mother had made special clothes for it. At school we played with dolls, juggled jacks with a small rubber ball, and often played an outdoor game called Red Rover, Red Rover let _____(name) come over. We jumped rope frequently and aimed to target our friends who were standing by the wall of a building with a rubber ball. If they were hit, they were "out!"

Art class was held in classrooms as the art teacher traveled from room to room. I remember one art assignment in first grade that was very perplexing to me. We were to draw a fruit bowl and I felt the task was too difficult for me. In my desperation, I must have whined or complained too much and suddenly she slapped my face. The whining stopped immediately – a lesson learned quickly and the hard way!

One of the competitive math contests I enjoyed and excelled was in fourth grade. My teacher, Miss Kuhn, flashed multiplication or addition flashcards as one student stood by another student's desk for some competition. The first person to respond quickly and correctly moved on to the next student. When my turn came, I kept on moving and winning until the competition ended. Much to my delight, I became the class winner. Later on, when I taught second grade, I tried the math flash card competition with my students. It was a challenge and an incentive to learn the basic math facts well, although, I sensed several students were reluctant to join the fun since they had not learned them well enough.

Our fifth grade teacher required us to memorize all the USA states and their corresponding capitals and eventually present them to the class from memory. When my turn came, I remember standing nervously to begin my recitation: Main-Augusta; New Hampshire-Concord; Vermont – Montpelier and that is as far as I can remember. Even today I wonder how beneficial it was to memorize all the fifty states and their capitals when there are available resources to search for the information if needed.

We respected our teachers. We studied judiciously, completed our assignments, and took our studies seriously. However, one middle school teacher was so strict that I was rather afraid of him. A disrespectful student was asked to stand tiptoe for minutes and stick her nose in a circle he had drawn on the blackboard until he released her. He once grabbed a student from her seat who was sitting across from me. I do not know what she had done to enact such discipline.

I must tell an interesting and unforgettable cookie story. A snack was expected when we arrived home from school. Mother baked good cookies and placed them in an aluminum kettle with a lid in the pantry which is a small room attached to the kitchen. One day I knew she had baked one of my favorite cookies – PEANUT BUTTER COOKIES! One rule we were obligated to follow was no snacks until 4:00! I wondered why it had to be at that exact time. It made no sense to me. Why couldn't it be at another time–maybe earlier? We also knew it was best to get permission to eat a cookie. One day Mother went outside to the building next to the house called the woodhouse since it stored lots of wood and two coal bins. I believed this was an excellent time to "steal" a cookie. I yielded to temptation and knew I had to hurry! I opened the pantry door, lifted the lid, removed ONE cookie with carefulness so as not to disarray the remaining cookies. The lid was replaced quickly and I detected no evidence that she would ever know there had been a "thief" in those forbidden cookies. I quickly munched down the peanut butter cookie without much enjoyment. I was more concerned she would return while I was in the process of "stealing and eating!" After I chewed and swallowed the cookie quickly, I wiped my mouth thoroughly, drank some water, and looked in the mirror to see if there was any evidence left of cookie crumbs anywhere. I felt absolutely SAFE! I walked into the living room and stood by one side of our Glow Boy coal stove while Mother stood on the other side as we visited. It wasn't long until I saw her twitching nose–something like a rabbit, and make a sniffing noise! I did not like what I saw or heard. Soon she said to me, "Did you have a cookie?" I told the truth and said, "Yes!" "How do you know?" I asked. Her reply was, "I smelled the peanut butter on your breath!" Unbelievable, I thought! I got caught in a way I never dreamed would happen. More important is the fact I was not afraid to tell the truth for she had told us that if we did so, she would not punish us. That was a mighty good lesson to learn and live by. In addition, I used this great nugget of truth and applied it in my own classroom. It worked! It released the fear of telling the truth!

MY HIGH SCHOOL EDUCATIONAL EXPERIENCES

While in high school, I wanted to play in the band and envisioned playing the clarinet, but Mother did not allow me to join because I would have to wear slacks and this was wrong according to her belief system. I did participate in the high school chorus and the music director was the same teacher that had given me a slap on my face during art class in first grade. I also helped sell candy bars at the candy counter. How I wished I had the money to purchase the enticing candy that I stared at every day. A high school classmate who worked with me at the counter always seemed to have money to buy candy. I wondered what that would be like to have cash to spend so freely. Whether I looked hungry or she believed I was poor, she shared her money with me so that I could select something sweet from the candy counter.

In high school we typed on electric typewriters and had one-minute and five-minute timed speed tests. I won pins for being "speedy!" It would have been wonderful to have had computer training but computers were not available then. I well remember substituting for a class and was amazed how the very young children knew how to use one. I virtually knew nothing about computers then. Now later in adult life, I still struggle how to use my computer efficiently and confidently. Being basically self-taught leaves unresolved computer issues and frustrations. There are obviously many more things to be learned.

UNDERGRADUATE AND POST GRADUATE
COLLEGE DEGREES

We did not attend kindergarten. From grade one through grade twelve, yearly incremental steps led me to high school graduation with a High School Diploma from Bremen High School in 1953 and entered Goshen College obtaining my BA (Bachelor of Arts) degree in Elementary Education licensed as a certified elementary teacher in 1956. Within five years of teaching, a school rule required a teacher to study for the MA (Masters Degree) that I obtained from Ball State University in 1962. Much later on I had encouragement from a Ball State professor to work on my doctorate. Taking several years to give it more thought, I enrolled as a doctoral student at Ball State University, Muncie, Indiana, and graduated the summer of 1975 with a major in Elementary Education, cognates in Reading and Special Education.

In the meantime, I taught second grade and later third and fourth grade students, assisted classroom teachers as a reading consultant and substituted for public school teachers. Teaching in five different colleges and universities provided a variety of experiences with adults.

I was constantly involved in private tutoring working with students from first grade to college. One-on-one tutoring sessions were usually very helpful and an encouraging to observe progress in many ways. I have often commented that my middle name should have been "Tutor!"

EDUCATION OF MY SIBLINGS

My older brother had no college education even though he aspired to be a doctor. My sister obtained her BS (Bachelor of Science) degree in nursing from Goshen College and my younger brother got his Ph.D. in organic chemistry from Northwestern University, Evanston, Illinois.

MY TEACHING EXPERIENCES

In my earlier years of teaching without a computer, my typing was done on mimeograph paper that had a carbon sheet on the back of it. When a mistake was made, a liquid called "White Out" could be used or I used a razor blade and scraped the error on the carbon copy and retyped over it. Finally, there was a certain kind of ribbon that could be installed in the typewriter and by backspacing, the error would be deleted. That was progress!

For a few more interesting teaching facts, elementary teachers always ate lunch at the same tables with their students. They were responsible to encourage students to eat their food and also have good behavior. Once I tried to encourage a student to eat the cooked spinach on his tray. After he vomited, I decided then that the parents were responsible for their children's eating habits – not the teachers! I asked another student to eat a certain food on his tray and the response was, "It doesn't look like my Mother's." I replied, "Did your Mother fix it?" We also went outside and supervised each recess – usually three in a day. We served on committees. I gave several presentations with some of my students for PTA (Parent-Teacher Association) while their parents attended the meetings. The largest class of second graders I had was 36 – way too many, I thought. We taught with no aides. There were parent-teacher conferences and one evening was designated for them. "Open House" meant to prepare your room with student displays and an open invitation was given for parents, friends, and relatives to attend.

One of the biggest challenges I faced in education was accepting the chairmanship and responsibilities of South Bend Teachers' Institute language arts division and plan for speakers, workshops, and displays. Some of my students helped with the program singing some of Lois Lenski's songs found in books that she had authored. I also introduced her to over 1,000 teachers in attendance. It was a rare occasion! It was a highlight of my career – something that initially I thought I could not do. In fact, she visited my home and took a pony cart ride with my Amish neighbor children. She also invited several other teachers and we celebrated lunch together.

For eight years I taught in a public school that was involved in the Title I reading and math governmental program. Students were tested to determine who would qualify for the program in reading. Throughout the day I met with a small group of students from grades 1 through 6 who had poor reading skills, and I soon realized there were other factors involved: low self-esteem; unnurtured home environment; behavioral problems; disinterest; poor attitudes; and failures that had become such a part of their lives. I was also responsible to help classroom teachers giving advice or answering questions. It was required to attend Title I meetings in Indianapolis too. According to the Title I Education rules, a lot of testing and paper work was necessary. Another requirement with the government program was to give parent workshops for those who had children enrolled in the Title I program. I learned a lot in those eight years determining what the children's reading problems were and assessing the best ways to overcome them. Observing their difficulties, assessing the quality of work, attitudes, and taking responsibility completing assignments were all considered in the "mixture" of how to remediate the problems. To determine what teaching methods were not helpful or those that had been neglected could be challenging.

For several years I helped with a government program, the NAEP (National Association of Educational Progress), testing students' abilities in reading and math in various public schools.

Providing workshops for teachers at various locations was another way to share ideas, answer questions, and interact with each other.

PONDERING EDUCATIONAL THOUGHTS

I felt it necessary to give a brief glimpse of my parent's little formal educational background, their contributions, and successes they made in so many ways compared with the educational opportunities my siblings and I had when we went to a public school and onto college. Our jobs required college degrees. I would like to share a few nuggets about education:

1. Study diligently and do your best.
2. Yearn to be successful.
3. Grab the opportunities to learn new skills.
4. Improve the knowledge and skills that you do have now.
5. Self-educating and learning never stop if there is a will to do it.
6. Quality learning experiences may make one more efficient than the quantity of years studying.

Chapter 6
A PRODUCTIVE WORK ETHIC

What does it take to have a productive work ethic? What factors may influence procrastinators or "workcoholics?" Can a work ethic be overdone and crowd out other important aspects of life? What determines the balance? When should children be given responsibilities?

A productive work ethic may well assimilate into the next generation as both my parents accomplished much by their modeling of constant and goal-oriented busyness both outdoors and indoors every day except Sunday. Working and keeping busy was expected of us as well: start a task, stay at it, and complete it. Do not procrastinate! Once I asked my youngest brother, Alan, "How did Mother and Father accomplish so much?" He replied, "They worked hard!"

FATHER'S RESPONSIBILITES

Father's major responsibilities outside the home were constructing buildings. He built barns, houses, a cattle barn, and repaired or made changes to other buildings upon request. In addition to the carpentry work, he had "at-home" responsibilities too. He filed saws for others as he sat by his pot-bellied stove in the garage. What fun we had placing the saw filings on top of a white sheet of paper while moving a magnet held underneath it. It was a fascinating at-home science lesson that helped to understand repelling and attracting magnetic poles. He spaded a large area for a garden with the help of my brother. A large "truck patch" was plowed by a neighbor as more home-grown produce would supply us with a variety of fresh organic foods. He used a large one-wheeled cultivator to loosen the soil and kill the weeds. It was our job to help hoe the weeds within the plant rows to keep them under control. No chemicals were used on our produce as they were GMO free!

Father had several beehives. He gave the bees special care as they were very valuable pollinators. He fed them extra sugar water during the winter months. They provided us with delicious raw honey in the comb. Bees are known to swarm and once it happened in our back yard. We heard a "chorus" of buzz-zzzing bee sounds that was a good indicator of swarming. Following the direction of the noise, we found them hanging together like a huge oriole's nest on a branch of our sweet cherry tree in the back yard. Father told us that when we saw a swarm, we should get two pan lids and clang them together so they will settle and remain on the branch. There was always the possibility they would leave before they were rescued. One day a swarming episode occurred, and I biked several miles to the place where my Father was working and told him he should come home immediately to rescue the swarm. He wore his protective bee garb after he came home and made a very important comment, "I have to be sure to get the queen to enter the beehive first so the other bees will follow." After the successful rescue, I was rewarded with twenty-five cents which seemed like a lot of money to me. I was happy that I followed Father's advice and helped save a bunch of swarming bees.

Many different kinds of fruit trees were planted on our over-an-acre property: peaches; sweet cherries; sour cherries; apples; plums; pears; apricots; and one messy mulberry tree. Insects were attracted to the fruit as it ripened. They knew where to find their "banquet of sweet treats. A large tank with prepared spray had handles and wheels that could be rolled along on the ground. A long sturdy stick was used as an improvised ladle to stir the ingredients containing sulphur. That was my job as Father sprayed the trees. One summer the fruit on the apricot trees looked black. Upon further examination, they were decked with unrelenting small black bugs! Finally, those two trees were removed and the "banquet" days for those bugs were over.

Many kinds of berries were picked on our property: black raspberries; strawberries; red currants; and gooseberries. One day I was asked to pick the raspberries and I was not in a good mood, but I knew that disobedience or complaining could reap unwanted consequences. Therefore, I started picking them. In the meantime, I prayed that God would send rain so I could stop. That is precisely what happened! Of course, delaying this unwanted job did not resolve the issue of getting it completed. After the "rain break," I knew I had to continue picking those berries.

Father also cut hair for a neighbor man who lived several miles north of us. His hair was cut with a pair of old hair clippers as he sat on a high stool on our west porch.

MOTHER'S RESPONSIBILITIES

Mother knew what it was like to work hard when she was growing up. She carried that work ethic into her married life and exhibited it to us. I will call it "productive busyness!" One did not see Mother without wearing an apron every day. Wearing aprons was the norm in those days. She was a great gardener and thoroughly enjoyed it. It was her delight to have an impeccable garden with a variety of healthy plants. She saved some of her seeds from year to year and planted those seedlings in her own garden. Thus, she had the kind of plants she wanted to keep from year to year. To provide neatly spaced straight rows in the garden, a contrived home-made contraption was "invented." It could be pushed along the soil with a handle, and each of the two wheels made a mark or guide in a row where the seeds were to be planted. One could find lots of vegetables planted: corn; squash; pickles; tomatoes; red beets; lettuce; broccoli; cabbage; ground cherries that were made into delicious pies; rhubarb; celery; asparagus; carrots; beans; peas; sweet potatoes; onions; and white potatoes. Sometimes I would use the garden hoe to dig out the weeds or use the small Troy built motorless cultivator between the rows. To control the potato bugs from devouring the plants, Mother would hold a tin can filled with gasoline to the "uninvited guests" and they would quickly fall into it and meet their death! If white butterflies were flying around the broccoli plants, that was a sign, "beware of worms," since no insecticides were used as a general rule. I enjoyed working outside and keeping a "perfect" looking garden that would not only please me but my hard-working mother too.

Food was usually canned in a "Conservo," an old fashion steamer, that can house fourteen quarts at one time. Apples, sweet corn, and pears were dried on a drying pan. They were specialties for us.

Over a hundred-year year old Concord grapevine provided many grapes to make grape juice, grape jam, and delicious grape pies. This beautiful grape arbor was also a unique setting for a family wedding.

Mother's work was not only outside but there were tasks inside the house as well. She was the cook with the apron in the kitchen preparing meals baking or cooking from "scratch." She was quite the experimenter often modifying the recipes a bit or trying new recipes hoping we would like them. She once told us, "I don't mind trying new recipes, but if you don't like them, eat them anyway." We soon learned that snoopiness would not work at our house. Going to the grocery store meant to buy only certain items we could not produce or make. It was more economical to raise your own food and prepare it even though it usually took longer. Buying food in packages or in aluminum cans was usually not necessary and avoided due to some unhealthy ingredients and processing.

She prepared a few unique or original foods from her own recipes: vinegar; sandwich spread; catsup; apple butter; fried crispy mush; and eggs baked in muffin tins lined with buttered cornflakes. Baked foods were special and tasty: oatmeal cookies; homemade doughnuts; cottage cheese with maple syrup; and delicious homemade sauerkraut. A special dessert was homemade butterscotch pudding with bananas, whipped egg whites, and sprinkled with nuts. Oatmeal was a basic ingredient in many foods: muffins; pancakes; bread; cookies with raisins; and baked whole wheat pudding eaten with butter and jelly or with fruit and milk. Dandelion greens were dug from our yard, cooked, and then boiled eggs and a sauce were added. Quality of food was a primary concern and I believe we grew up eating quite healthy. Without a doubt, the kitchen for Mother was a very busy place. It must have been the Hochstetler Family Restaurant!

Now you can go to a grocery store and purchase prepared foods in bags, cans, and bottles. The quality may be questionable as ingredients listed on labels are often unfamiliar, some unpronounceable, and may not be found in the dictionary. These foods may be fast and convenient but not necessarily healthy. Many products are pasteurized to protect us from bacterial infections but may lessen essential nutrients. Some of the labels, however, contain the word "fortified." Preparation takes much less time and requires little knowledge except to understand the directions and follow them. This type of eating may well cause some of our health issues today.

Woolen sweaters and blankets were protected with moth balls placed in a cedar chest so that moths would not chew holes in them. Blankets were often aired yearly on the outdoor clothesline too.

For three years she wrote weekly airmail letters to my brother, Alan, who was in Vietnam and Korea. This took a lot of discipline to accomplish writing the long-detailed letters. He kept those letters in a shoebox and since his death, we have saved them among other items.

WORK ETHIC SUMMARY

My Father always had a job to do. He did not charge as much as other construction workers. He was skilled in building anything neighboring people needed. Mother was also skilled in so many ways to provide for our family and she took it seriously. She was quite knowledgeable about food issues. People would call her for advice on food related topics. One could consider my parents "perfectionists" as their work was always neatly done.

The work ethic was such a part of their lives and it was "modeled" for us. We were expected to work without complaining. There were no monetary rewards unless it was merited in some way. Today the work ethic seems to have gone somewhat "with the wind" or "down the tube." I observed this in my own classroom and teachers still find it a struggle to cope with irresponsible students today. A good work ethic does not begin in adult life.

There is an old appropriate adage: "All work and no play make Jack a dull boy!" I am very thankful for the rich working heritage that has been part of my life. I still desire to work the best I can and enjoy it!

Chapter 7
THE MULLTI-PURPOSE BUSY KITCHEN

C an you imagine a house without a kitchen? Why is the kitchen such a busy place? How differently would we function without dishwashers, microwaves, electric beaters, food processors, Vita Mixes, and Turbo ovens? Is our health conditioned as to the kinds of food prepared in our kitchens?

THE KITCHEN WITH SEVEN DOORS AND TWO WINDOWS

Come with me and live in the house where we grew up that dates back to the 1870's. Perhaps you can draw a picture of the layout in your mind or on paper. It is a four-story house with an attic, upstairs, downstairs, and cellar as we called it. There were seven doors and two windows in the kitchen before it was remodeled. The east door opened to a very large garden and building we called the woodhouse that stored twigs and wood, two coal bins, garden implements, and a large container of chicken mash. Another building to the east was our chicken house. The two-car garage further east was the home for Father's Model T Ford and later for a 1936 four-door Chevrolet. Much later on, a brand-new red Dodge truck was purchased to accommodate the carpenter tools.

The main west kitchen door led to our wooden porch with several steps, a large truck patch, and part of the yard with a huge old sugar maple tree and a pine tree that provided much shade during the hot summer months and a refuge for many different kinds of birds.

The south part of the kitchen had two doors. The pantry stored these items: the motorized wringer washing machine; several shelves of different sized bowls; a few kerosene lamps since there was no electricity at the time; and a cupboard with extra pans and dishes. The other door was a closet for storage: an ironing board; a copper boiler; every day coats; a washboard to scrub dirty clothes; a shelf for rags; a clothes basket for dirty clothes; and a pot.

The kitchen floor was difficult to clean since the light-colored linoleum became dirty from the wood/coal burning stove. I can well remember getting down on my hands and knees on a knee pad with a pail of hot water, a cloth, and a scrub brush to clean the floor. Scouring powder was also used in spots where the dirt was difficult to remove. It was a lot of weekly scrubbing on Saturday. Later on, a better kind of linoleum was purchased and the coal stove was removed. From then on, the floor was so much easier to clean.

The north part of the kitchen had two doors. One of them led to our cellar that had lots of cupboards and shelves with canned food from our garden and truck patch and an ice box to keep some foods refrigerated. A sign was placed in one window indicating to the "ice man" how many pounds of ice (in chunks) he should leave. He carried the cold, icy, chunk down the cellar steps. Food was stored in the top part of the ice box and ice in the lower part. An ice box was obviously not as efficient as a refrigerator but it was better than nothing. Because there was no electricity and, therefore, no refrigerator, left-over food was sometimes reheated to prevent spoilage. It was certainly not frugal to waste food and allow it to spoil. We ate left-overs even if bread was mixed with it to make a larger quantity.

There was also a potato bin in the cellar. As we dug our potatoes, they were put in the bin to store, but eventually, the rapidly growing sprouts had to be broken off – a job we had while sitting in the bin.

The other north door was left open to walk into our two "living quarters." This door had window panes and a window shade. It closed for our weekly Saturday baths. Before there was a bathroom, baths were taken in a large galvanized tub filled with water from the wood/coal stove's reservoir and from water heated in two large teakettles. The oven door of the stove was sometimes opened to allow more heat to warm the kitchen if necessary. Kitchen doors were locked and window shades were drawn to provide privacy.

Growing up without a bathroom meant that we had to walk up a sidewalk to a one-seater outdoor toilet that was supplied with toilet paper and a hooked door. There was also a pot stored in the closet and the person who used it last was responsible to empty it before retiring for bed.

Some years later, Father constructed and modernized our first small bathroom by remodeling the north end of the west porch. The bathroom had two doors, a toilet stool, electric lights, a fan, a lavatory, a bathtub, and a small window. It was a time of celebration, appreciation, and thankfulness. To take a bath or shower in a bathroom was indeed luxurious at this house. Another change has been made to the bathroom since 1991. The door from the kitchen to the bathroom has been closed to allow more space in the kitchen.

WASH DAY IN THE KITCHEN

Monday was washday in the kitchen. Some of the men's dirtiest work clothes were soaked first and scrubbed with a washboard if necessary before they were put in the washing machine as we called it. Mother made sure that the coal and wood stove was heated to provide very hot water for the copper boiler that was placed on top of the stove to be used primarily to presoak the white clothes before they were placed in the washing machine. Naphtha soap or chunks of homemade soap containing lye with perfume were used to wash the clothes until the detergent, Tide, was purchased in a box with a drinking glass in it. Water was pumped from pumps in the kitchen and sometimes from a pump outside and carried in a pail to the house filling the washing machine and the two rinse tubs. After the clothes were sorted, all the white clothes were first removed from the boiler. The water was so hot that a strong short stick or pole was used to lift them out into a deep dishpan and then dumped into the washing machine. Each pile of clothes was washed and then put through the wringer into the first tub of rinse water unless it was drip-dry material. Next, they were put through the wringer again into the second tub of water containing bluing that helped to keep the white clothes retain their "white" color.

The bluing granules were in a small tied bag but eventually were purchased in boxes or bottles. With one more "trip" through the wringer, the clothes were hung on an outdoor clothesline or on a rope-type clothesline in the house during inclement weather. The rope was strung carefully around nails at strategic places. After the washing was finished, the rinse water was carried to the garden pail by pail to give the home-grown celery much needed extra water during the summer.

The kitchen stove had a reservoir that kept the water warm by burning coal or corncobs. A damper controlled a movable plate or valve in the flue or stove pipe to control the draft. I remember Mother pouring some kerosene from a container on the wood or corn cobs to get a fire started in the stove. Of course, ashes accumulated and were carried outside and put in our not-so-deep-ditch on our lawn beside the road.

Another advantage of having such a warm stove was to put our wet mittens and gloves on a shelf near the chimney that dried them quite well when we played in the snow. Sometimes the oven door was opened to warm our cold feet.

GETTING WATER WITH HAND PUMPS

There was no running water from a spigot. Instead, there were two hand pumps, one rain water and one drinking water on each side of the steel sink in the kitchen. They were not the best pumps since they required a lot of exertion to get a substantial amount of water. Hands were washed in a wash basin kept in the sink, and our tooth brushes hung on hooks. A homemade linen towel hung on a hook to wipe our hands. The drinking water was collected from the pump in the kitchen or from a deep outside well. The pail of water was then carried into the kitchen and placed on the cabinet. A water dipper and a ladle were used to fill our glasses. These pumps also provided our bath water as well as the warm water in the wood stove's reservoir. Water was heated to wash dishes in dish pans. I remember a storm that produced a lot of lightning. While we were eating at the kitchen table one evening, a bolt of lightning must have struck the pumps or the metal around the sink as we saw the sparks fly! It was a scary moment.

WASHING DISHES IN DISHPANS

Since there was no kitchen sink available to wash dishes, three dish pans were the substitutes. Dishes were washed in the first pan, rinsed in the second pan, and allowed to drain in the third one. Hot water was heated in teakettles and homemade soap or Tide was used to wash them. Homemade dish towels were often made from feed bag material. Sometimes it was embarrassing for me to have guests at our house because we washed dishes from pans. The thought occurred to me: "Do they think we are "backwards" or poor? I remember wishing so much we had a better way to wash them and many years later, the new kitchen had a convenient modern sink.

IRONING WRINKLED CLOTHES

Of course, ironing time was after washday. Clothes that went through the wringer several times had a lot of wrinkles. Four old fashioned flat irons were heated on the kitchen stove and were used alternately held by a thick pad on the iron's handle to protect our hands from getting burned while we were ironing. Once the iron was not hot enough, it was replaced with another heated iron. A sprinkling bottle filled with water was "spritzed" on the clothing to provide more moisture to remove the wrinkles. Men's white starched shirt collars required careful ironing.

LIVING WITH A KEROSENE STOVE AND LAMPS

In addition to the wood/coal stove in the kitchen, there was also a kerosene stove with several burners that needed to be lit with a match before they were used. This stove was used to dry apples, pears, and sweet corn on a drying pan. The dried sweet corn was a delicacy. Eventually, it was replaced with a natural gas stove with four burners and an oven. This was definitely an advancement and improvement for our kitchen for which we were thankful. Several kerosene lamps were used to provide light during the dark evenings in the kitchen and living room. The wicks of these lamps would need occasional trimming so the flames would burn more evenly. I can still "smell" the offensive odor of these lamps!

PREPARING AND CANNING FOOD IN THE KITCHEN

Preparing and canning produce from our garden and truck patch made the kitchen not only a busy area of our house but a most welcomed and visited place too. Lots of food was canned in Ball quart jars that we labeled and dated. Meat was canned that had been ground into hamburger. There were delicious cracklings to eat as we helped with the canning process. After the lids had been securely sealed, the jars were taken to the cellar and put in cupboards. So, our winter supply of food was always nearby.

A few interesting facts about canning and can lids began when Pasteur discovered bacteria in the mid 1800's and there was emphasis on improving canning procedures by 1958. Mason invented a jar which allowed a metal cap to be screwed onto it. In 1902, Kerr invented the Kerr lids and by 1914 they had a rubber sealing gasket attached to them. Today food can be canned with separate lids and rings free of BPA. Ball and Kerr regular or wide mouth canning jars can be purchased. There are special glass jars that can be used to freeze food. What progress!

It was the eating place around the kitchen table that we all enjoyed: good cooking; fresh homemade bread; fried mush; delicious cookies; and popped popcorn. Making popcorn balls and homemade fudge were special food items. It did not matter if the kitchen was not modern according to standards today. We accepted the fact that this was our way of life.

One of the special pleasantries was to make homemade dough-nuts with Mother's guidance. Dough was rolled out with a wooden rolling pin and then the doughnuts were cut with a doughnut cutter. We pulled the kitchen table up to the kettle with the hot oil on the stove. One by one each doughnut was placed very carefully into the very hot oil and remained there until it became a shade of light brown. They were then removed from the kettle and rolled into sugar to add sweetness. We still talk about these memorable experiences today.

My brother, Alan, and I liked to eat cookie batter with a spoon. We asked Mother to leave some extra batter in the bowl. To make sure that we each got equal portions of what was left, she made a dividing line through the middle of the bowl–one section for him and one for me. Our wise Mother knew what she should do to avoid an argument if one had more batter to eat or one strayed from his side too far. We looked forward to having a good "licking" time!

OTHER FOOD TIDBITS

Potatoes were cooked to make mashed potatoes. No electric mixer was used. Instead, a hand-held metal potato masher that had holes in it was used to "stomp" the potatoes well. Gravy tasted good on top of them.

There were no built-in kitchen cupboards. There was no space for them unless the kitchen would be remodeled in some way. So, one Coppes kitchen cupboard painted white took the place of built-in cupboards. It contained our everyday dishes, silverware, a sugar bowl, drinking glasses, a bread box, a bread board, a long door for other items, and a lower door for storing food.

Bushels of red and yellow delicious apples were wrapped individually in pages of Sears Roebuck Catalog and placed in old empty nail kegs which were then stored under the kitchen at ground level where it stayed cooler for the winter months. We often ate apples on Sunday evening while Mother peeled them.

Homemade sauerkraut was an excellent tasty food that took a lot of preparation. After the cabbage was shredded and salted, it was put in a large crock covered with a plate. A stone was placed on top of the plate to produce weight so the fermenting process would stay inside the crock. Occasionally the foam had to be removed that collected at the top. A cloth that was tied with old nylon hosiery was placed on top of the crock. The entire process took at least a week to ten days to complete. It was important to keep checking it.

PROGRESSION OF KITCHEN CONTRIVANCES

Thinking back of the progression of handy kitchen contrivances from long ago, a few came to my mind:

1. from wood/coal/ kerosene stoves, central heating and air conditioning
2. mix by hand, hand held mixer, and bowl with electric beaters
3. flat irons, steam irons, and drip-dry materials with no pressing needed
4. hand wash, gas engine washer with wringer, and electric washer

5. reheat food, icebox, refrigerator, freezer
6. candles, kerosene lamps, battery operated lamps, electric ones
7. Glow Boy stove, floor furnace, central heating furnace

INVOLVING OTHERS IN THE KITCHEN
ESPECIALLY CHILDREN

1. Children can help prepare simple meals by following verbal or written directions with adult guidance.
2. The kitchen may be a time to prepare meals, set the table, and in the meantime socialize. This gives them an opportunity to take responsibility for a worthy cause.
3. Clean up time is part of kitchen duties whether it be the table or the floor.
4. Family members could prepare food for an elderly couple, a shut-in, a neighbor, or someone who needs assistance.
5. Try new recipes and follow the directions closely. Ingredients need to be available which is part of planning.
6. There are recipes for non-bake cookies and other easy-to-make dishes.

These ideas can be incorporated in a helpful way utilizing the interest, skills, and needs to involve family.

Chapter 8
SEWING, CLOTHING, BEDS, TOTE BAGS, AND RELATED PROJECTS

W e grew up during the Depression years that had a considerable impact on how we lived. We wore mostly homemade clothes with some variations in material and design. Patterns could be purchased in stores to sew dresses, for example. Now it seems much easier and simpler to visit stores to buy what is accessible, use mail-order catalogs, or on-line options. Special effort should be made to check the labels. Have you noticed where your clothing and other products were manufactured? You may be wearing clothes made from China, Malaysia, and Indonesia all at one time. How many USA labeled items do you wear?

Is there a lack of interest in sewing? Is it cheaper to buy clothes especially on sale than it is to buy materials, buttons, zippers, lace and other accessories? Are people too busy with other jobs and interests to engage in sewing, knitting, crocheting and quilting?

SEWING HOMEMADE CLOTHES
The White Singer treadle sewing machine that is at least three generations old still operates efficiently in our household. It was in constant use and had utmost care when Mother was still living. Most of our clothes were made on this sewing machine during our growing-up years.

Material was purchased and often stored in cupboards until needed. Mother was the primary sewer or seamstress. New patterns were available to purchase with a variety of designs although they often had to be modified for us. Mother's dresses were usually the same pattern or style with collars, buttons or zippers down the front, and three-quarter length sleeves.

OTHER TYPES OF CLOTHING

Mother was adept in making winter coats and caps for her four grandchildren who were all boys. While in high school, Mother made our athletic outfits. She did not think that "gym suits" were modest enough that were sold at the school. We could wear socks or anklets as we called them but only for gym class. Once I wore a pair of anklets home from school and Mother was unhappy. She did not believe they should be worn elsewhere, but eventually, she accepted it.

My sister, Mary Ellen, remembers having three cotton school dresses while she was in elementary school wearing one dress for three consecutive days and another one two consecutive days. The third dress was then worn at the beginning of the next week. She had a classmate that had a ready-made brown skirt with pockets and often had pretzels in one of them. She assumed that they must be quite rich to buy clothes.

She began sewing when she was a freshman in high school and continued to make many dresses, skirts, blouses, and a coat. The dresses were made in similar styles but varied with materials, buttons, zippers, lace, and ruffles. She made her own nurse's uniforms when she was working in a doctor's office. She also made a suit, slacks, shirts, a leisure jacket, and a necktie for her husband. Another sewing project was to use brown and white small checked material to make Edna a blouse and matching shirts for her husband, Dean, and their four boys. A leather jacket was made for him too. Buttonholes were handmade using a buttonhole scissors. A threaded needle stitched the edges of the buttonhole since the old Singer sewing machine did not have this kind of an attachment. She also enjoyed making at least 40 or more beautiful adult and baby comforters from scrap material!

A STRICT DRESS CODE

Mother was strict with precise dress measurements. The length of the dress had to be well below the knees, the sleeves were to reach the elbows, and the neck should not be cut too low. Modesty was the key. So, our school and Sunday dresses and skirts were similar in pattern. During this time, we were also told it was wrong to wear anything resembling men's clothing such as slacks or jeans since the Bible stated that women should not wear men's clothing. One can refer to the following scripture verse: *"Deuteronomy 22:5 – "The woman shall not wear that which pertaineth unto a man, neither shall a man put on a woman's garment: for all that do so are an abomination unto the Lord the God."* It would not be modest to wear shorts either.

MAKING CLOTHES AND CURTAINS
FROM CHICKEN FEED SACKS

Chicken feed came in bags with simple colorful designs or plain and the material was quite durable. After the feed was out of the bag, it was washed, dried, and ready for use. Some of our underclothes were made from these bags and dyed pink. I am not sure why they had to be pink, but it satisfied us! Some of the colorful feed bags were made into pajamas and plain ones for bed sheets. Kitchen curtains with designs helped to decorate the kitchen in a unique way. Pillow slips with floral designs were on our beds. Some had embroidered designs with the open edges crocheted using matching yarn to make them more attractive.

WEARING CLOTHING ACCESSORIES

Wearing jewelry was not acceptable in our background from a biblical and Mennonite perspective. So pins, necklaces, and bracelets were not worn. It was simply wrong to do so based on *I Peter 3:3: "Whose adorning let it not be the outward adorning of plaiting the hair, and of wearing gold, or of putting on of apparel."* Simplicity and modesty were the criteria to follow and deviating from them was wrong! Today jewelry and slacks are worn and hair is cut. It no longer seems wrong!

A STITCH IN TIME SAVES NINE

Mother believed not only in being thrifty but wearing an article of clothing as long as possible. The slogan seemed to be: "Don't buy a new one or throw it away, but rather mend, darn, or sew on a patch." This included darning socks, sewing patches on torn knee pants, mending any holes regardless of size, and anything that needed repair. One neighbor lady commented that she had never seen a woman that could sew patch upon patch as Mother did in reference to the patches she saw on my younger brother's pants. I am not sure if that was a compliment but she definitely was amazed. There was also a wicker rocking chair that was repaired in our living room. The apparent philosophy was: "Fix what needs fixing. Use what you have as long as you can. Don't spend money on something new when it is not necessary." Thus, this old adage was upheld in our household: "A stitch in time saves nine!"

CREATIVE PROJECTS

When Mother read about a creative idea in magazines or other resources, it was an incentive for her to try it. During the process, she might modify it in some way. Mother's creative projects included: braiding small rugs from colorful strips that were cut from left-over pieces of double-knit material; making a unique tote bag by cutting strips from red and white striped bread wrappers; and sewing over one hundred tote bags from left over scraps of upholstery. An inner lining was made for the bags and their pockets, and the handles were reinforced. The quality of material was durable with varied colors and designs. These bags were not only attractive and beautiful but were very practical and usable. They made beautiful gifts. I sold many to teachers and acquaintances. She also made: dish towels; dish rags; hand towels; and square or circular hot pads from scrap materials.

Quilting was a practical and useful way to use leftover scrap pieces of material that were cut into a variety of shapes, colors, and designs. Our meticulous Mother made one beautiful quilt for her hospital bed that required 840 small squares. Quilts were also made from colorful feed sacks and designed by the quilter using commercial stencils. Watching Mother and my step-grandmother stitching small neatly handmade stiches over and over on a quilt created a desire for me to make my own quilts–twelve double and queen size embroidered quilts and one with yellow and lavender pansy appliques. A binding with a matching color was sewed around the edges of the quilts. Almost all of them were sold or given to friends. A few were made upon request.

Quilting projects were a delightful project for me. There were many quilt selections to choose from while browsing through catalogs. I wished I could make all of them.

Monthly church quilting gatherings named "the sewing" involved mostly older women. These quilts were usually made and donated for relief purposes under the auspices of Mennonite Relief Sale or Mennonite Central Committee. The person who purchased the quilt at the relief sale was, in essence, donating money to help needy people. In addition, Amish women also quilted for their families and relief purposes as well.

AN UNUSUAL BED AND BED MATTRESS

My Father made a wooden framed bed that we still have in the attic. It is an irregular size – not single, double, king, or queen. Mattresses are difficult to find that will fit the bed properly. The bed sides have grooved notches every so often for wooden slats to be placed. The purchased metal spring is placed next giving it support for the mattress on top of it. The bed is hardly twin size and too small for two people. Once when my brother, Alan, was sleeping in this bed, a slat broke and he found himself partly out of bed! A repair job was badly needed!

My two brothers slept in a bed with a corn husk mattress. Unfortunately, it had to be fluffed regularly since the husk would move around, slip or clump together. One could hear the rustling of the corn husks as our hands were used to spread them into all sections of the mattress. In addition, a bumpy mattress was not comfortable physically and psychologically. I was glad when another more "modern" mattress replaced that one.

We had pillows that were stuffed with chicken feathers. The feathers were cleaned first, of course. Feathered pillows may carry allergens that can cause problems for some people. We used whatever was available.

STOCKINGS WORN LONG AGO

Nylon stockings had seams that were to be worn straight down the back of each leg. Sometimes it was a bit difficult to keep them straight as the seams might shift while wearing them. No decent lady wanted to be seen with a crooked seam! It was a wonderful day when seamless hosiery or stockings as we called them became available. Hosiery was held in place by wearing a garter belt with attached garters that were fastened onto the hosiery. The next best improvement was the marketing of the seamless pantyhose all in one piece.

MORE REFLECTION

One can hardly fathom the changes in clothing, shoes, and accessories while browsing through isles in stores, catalogs, and on line. Retailers have to lure customers to their products through attractiveness, stunning displays, discounts, and bargains with "For Sale" signs. Variations in sizes, colors, and designs are there to satisfy your personal taste and need, assure you to buy on credit, lay away, or purchase something – maybe unnecessarily. Another factor is to decide if the price is within your budget. By sewing clothes, we do not need to read signs that say "on sale," "50% discount," "clearance," "bargain table," or other discounted items.

Just wondering: How would people react if they were required to live back in the days when clothes were made from chicken sacks, homemade clothing was worn, and style was somewhat disregarded since it was not a necessity?

Has creativity been minimized or lost among many people living in the United States because everything is easily accessible and takes less time to buy it than make it? To those who are conscious of style, is it easier to sort through a variety of options on a rack or shelf? Is it more frugal to buy or make it? Keep on pondering!

Chapter 9

FROM HORSE DRAWN BUGGIES TO ELECTRIC AUTOMOBILES

Horse-drawn buggies or carriages were the speediest means of transportation on gravel roads long time ago. There are still people today who use this mode of travel and bicycles. I live in a community that is very familiar with the clippity-clop of horses' hooves pelting against the pavement. The changes that have occurred in cars from horse-drawn buggies have been monumental during out life time. I think back of our Mother telling us how she ran down their long lane to see the first car drive down the road in Nappanee, Indiana. My Mother told us she used to drive a car until she drove into a ditch. That incident kept her from ever driving a car again. So that left our Father to be the driver.

Vehicles with four wheels have lessened the need to walk, bike, or travel with a horse and buggy. So, what would it be like:

1.   To have only a horse-drawn buggy for travel?
2.   To drive with no heater in the car during the winter?
3.   To drive a car without turn signals especially in heavy traffic?
4.   To have no road or driving rules and regulations on our speedy highways and toll roads?
5.   To have no speed limits? While my brother, sister, and I were traveling in Europe, we traveled on the Autobahn with no

speed limits. My brother said he felt he had to use his rear-view mirror to drive safely. It was quite an experience.

MODERN CARS AND CONVENIENCES

I can remember the time when I could name the brand name of a car I saw on the street or highway. But that is no longer the case. Different kinds of brand names, sizes, colors, and improved interior devices are available today. Electric cars are now being assembled. There are heaters, air conditioners, GPS systems to use rather than maps or atlases, compasses, turn signals, mirrors, radios, CD players, temperature and gas gauges, protective air bags, cruise controls, and different speeds for windshield wipers. Seat belts are required to wear and if not adhered to can result in penalties. People use their cell phones and text while driving which has become a controversial topic for the safety and legal system. With varying speed limits posted on our highways and toll roads, drivers often exceed the speed limit.

Years ago, gas station attendants came to your car to fill the gas tank, clean the windshield, and put air in the tires if needed. Payment was made in cash while staying in your car. Those are by-gone days! Now there are self-serve stations. We do not have to wash our own cars and wax them at home since car washes can wash and give a polish job for a reasonable price. Coupons can be purchased at car washes that provide discounts. Credit cards are frequently used. At some stations, payment must be made for gas before filling the tank lest some run-away person takes off without paying. Gas prices seem to fluctuate a lot like a yo-yo and unpredictably day by day or within a day. One may check several gas stations for the cheapest price. The preferred brand of gas may not be available. So, you may try another time hoping for more satisfaction. The government has attempted to pass manufacturing laws to lessen the amount of pollution that the gas guzzling cars emit through their exhaust systems. Too many contaminates affect the very air that we breathe, and the newer cars are required to accommodate those restrictions.

DAYS OF THE MODEL T FORD

My Father drove an old Model T Ford and did not have to be concerned about all the current rules and regulations. He had to crank it by hand to start the motor. He drove it slowly and carefully-no more than thirty miles per hour, to his construction sites. One could hear the Model T Ford coming almost a mile from home. When he would honk the "ooga-ooga" sound of the horn, we knew he was not far away. In fact, we would have time to run out to the road, stand nearby, and put up our thumb like tramps used to do to signal we wanted a ride. He would stop, let us jump onto the rumble seat, and drive with him to the garage. Finally, the old Model T Ford was sold and a Dodge truck was purchased that could haul his carpenter tools in a compartmentalized homemade tool chest.

OUR 1936 FOUR-DOOR CHEVROLET

Father also had a 1936 four-door Chevrolet that was considered our family car when we went to town, church, or another family activity. Interesting descriptions of this car are as follows: a running board on both sides; no seatbelts; no heater to keep us warm so an army blanket was kept in the car to give us warmth; gear shift on the floor that moved to different positions using the clutch to get to the desired driving mode; no turn signals so the extended hand or arm signaled which direction through the open driver's window; bright/dimmer switch with a button like knob on the left side of the floorboard and to change it, the left foot stomped on that "knob" forcibly; no radio; and no CD player or GPS.

The Chevrolet was kept reasonably clean and Father had us wash, wax, and polish the car yearly. According to him, Simonize was the best brand to use. There was none other. We got paid twenty-five cents for helping, and we were happy with a little reimbursement!

This car serviced the Hochstetler family for a long time. Father believed in driving and taking care of it until a change had to be made. I have often wondered what would happen to my Father's 36 Chevrolet today would he be driving on one of our highways, especially toll roads, at his maximum speed of thirty miles per hour! Then, too, how would the younger generation of today cope with a Model T Ford, a 1936 Chevrolet, and all the inconveniences or fewer devices available compared with "modernized" vehicles?

When I was riding with my Father in the front seat of the car, he would allow me to steer it. Sometimes I wondered what it would be like to drive one! I found out after graduating from college. My first car was a second-hand Ford that had a "straight stick." Learning to drive it with both a clutch and a brake provided some jolts and rough starts until the shifting was developed with more expertise. Cars with gear shifts near the wheel and no clutch make driving so much easier today. There was also a written driver's test taken every four years. To obtain a driver's license at age 16 or older, a supervisor sat in the front passenger seat as you showed your alertness and ability to follow driving rules. You hoped you passed all the tests and were now an accomplished and safe driver.

A FEW MORE THOUGHTS OF THEN AND NOW

1. Many years ago, buying gas cost twenty-three cents a gallon!
2. Buying gas would enable one to accumulate green stamps to be used at your own discretion.
3. Vehicles had to go through inspection over a period of time. If everything was satisfactory, a sticker was placed on the upper left side of the windshield.
4. A driver's manual could be studied to pass the written driver's test.
5. License plates had to be purchased at your county's courthouse. Now one can obtain a yearly license plate by answering certain questions and making payment on line or by phone.
6. To renew your license plate today, it is required to have several sources of identification. *You have to prove YOU ARE YOU!*
7. How safe do you feel on our roads today? Why do people need to drive so fast?
8. Our highways may be more dangerous not only because of speeding, texting, and other distractable moments but with drunken drivers and those on illicit drugs or overdoses.
9. How often do we take the time to take leisurely rides through the country to enjoy moments of nature's "refreshments?" Is it safe to drive slowly?

Chapter 10
INEXPENSIVE PLAY-TIME ACTIVITIES

Think about these questions: Do children enjoy playing with expensive store-boughten toys rather than simple homemade ones? What other activities could adults make available for their children other than watching television? Are children too engrossed and involved in hand-held gadgets that diminish their creativity and imagination? Are adults encouraging or limiting children's imaginary, creative interests, and skills today? What games did you play when you were a young child?

INDOOR ACTIVITIES
Even though our parents had a strong work ethic, there was time for play indoors and outdoors. Most of the fun involved creativity and imagination without spending money at a toy store. So, let's first take a look at a variety of simple inexpensive indoor activities that we enjoyed:

1. A table board game called "Uncle Wiggly" allowed several people to play with red and yellow instructional cards or numbers to determine how many steps one should move. There were characters and places you hoped to avoid landing on their space. It could be "losing a turn or two" when approaching "Skeezix" who can trap you from moving ahead next time. It is a competitive game to see who can reach "home" first. The game can still be purchased on line today.

2. A box of Lincoln logs provided many moments of constructing buildings and bridges. My second grade classroom boys preferred to play with small pieces of wood that I had gotten from Ayr Cabinet at no cost. They enjoyed Tinker Toys that could be assembled as vehicles running on wheels. Legos would be another example.

3. A home-made wooden marble apparatus brought a lot of fascination by dropping one marble at a time into a slot that had enough momentum to follow all the zigzag narrow boards and land in its designated attached box. Different colored marbles could be dropped quickly into the slot to captivate attention.

4. Chinese checkers was another homemade marble board game. A dice and ten marbles were required to be placed at your home spot. Five players could play at one time. Each time the dice was thrown, the player moved that many places. If a player landed on your spot, that marble was sent back to the original place as a penalty. The goal was to go around the board reaching "home" first with all your marbles.

5. A competitive game of jacks that takes a lot of skill can be played with one or more persons. Ten jacks are scattered on a table or floor with one hand. Then a small rubber ball is bounced on the table/floor while grabbing one jack with the other hand without touching any of the others. Next, the ball is bounced again and two jacks are picked up without touching any others. The game is continued in this sequential manner until all ten have been picked up successfully. Penalties for inaccurate playing consist of touching jacks out of sequence and picking up too many or not enough at one time. If any of these occur, your turn has ended and all the jacks are given to the next player. It is wise to analyze the best way to grab the number needed each time so that the rules are followed and that the player can continue longer. The goal is to pick up ten jacks as quickly as possible with the fewest penalties to become the winner. One can soon learn that bouncing the ball forcibly will make it go higher and will allow a bit more time to pick up jacks.

6. A homemade board had ten indentations and a marble was placed in each one of them. That place was called "home" for each of the five players. Each player chose the same color for all his ten marbles such as all red, blue or green. The game was called "Aggravation" and held to its name! A dice was thrown and a player moved his marble the number of spaces the dice indicated. The goal of each player was to get all of his marbles back "home" safely. However, along the way another player could land on a spot where there was another player's marble and send it back to the beginning to start over again. It was sometimes truly an **aggravation** as one could find it difficult to advance successfully.

7. We had coloring books and crayons and often colored at the kitchen table. Mother was at our mercy when we colored. We would often ask her, "What color should we make this?" Why we could not make our own decision is still unknown to me. I still maintain a bump on one of the fingers on my right hand from coloring so much.

8. A small box of stencils with a variety of animals and other objects provided us with unlimited activity marking the slits in the stencils on paper with a pencil, connecting those slits, and then coloring the pictures that are formed.

9. Anagram letters were arranged to form specific words. It necessitated spelling each word correctly. I do not recall that we had any specified rules.

10. Using our imagination and ingenuity, chairs were laid down one after the other on the floor and covered with throw rugs to create a "tunnel" effect. We would then crawl through it until we reached the end.

11. My sister and I each had a doll without hair. Because we knew our parents would not buy us another doll, we improvised an unprofessional "beauty salon" with our own creative styling methods. Lined notebook paper was used to cut narrow strips. Each strip was wrapped around a pencil to form a curl. Many of these curls were made to give the dolls plenty of "hair" which were then taped onto their heads. Mother made colorful and well-fitting doll clothes, and I still cherish my special doll!

OUTDOOR ACTIVITIES

1. Our older brother, Dean, had a pair of stilts that consisted of a pair of poles with each one having a footrest somewhere along its length where each foot was placed. Once the feet were in place, an attempt was made to walk with them and remain in a balanced position. Just getting situated on them properly without falling was a "miracle!"

2. Hopscotch was one of our favorite games. To state generally, it consists of drawing one to ten large squares with chalk on the sidewalk with each one numbered consecutively. A suitable object is then thrown on a square by a player who hops the squares to pick up the object and continues until an error is made. The object is then returned to the next player. Different objects can be used: a stone, beanbag, button, plastic toy, or a bottle cap. There are some penalties. For more detailed instructions, refer to the Internet.

3. My sister and I took turns walking and leading each other blindfolded anywhere on our property. We would then need to guess the exact spot or location when we stopped. As I think back, I do not know why this was fun.

4. There was a sandbox underneath our large maple tree by the porch. I do not remember playing much in the sand when we were very young.

5. A children's wagon without sides and one wheel without rubber made a noisy sound that we disregarded as we pushed and pulled each other up and down the sidewalk. It was not important to us how much noise our wagon made. The neighbors could ignore it!

6. Two sleds, a metal and a wooden one, were available to use during the snowy winter months. Steering them properly was not always easy. In fact, I do not believe we used them very often, especially the wooden one.

7. "Kick the tin can" was one of our favorite games. A tin can was placed on the cement and kicked hard by a player while the other players ran quickly to find a hiding place. The "can kicker" then went on a spree in an attempt to find all the players. In the meantime, a player could kick the can again if he should feel

free enough to do it without getting caught. I do not remember how it was determined who would be the next "can kicker." Perhaps it was the first person that was caught hiding. Maybe your own rule could suffice here.

8. "Andy Over" consisted of two teams, one team on each side of a building, which was usually our house. A person on Team 1 tried to throw the ball over the roof to Team 2. If the ball went to the other side, the player announced "Andy Over" and anyone on that side would try to catch the ball and win a point. They would then throw it back to Team 1 and announce "Andy Over" again. If someone on Team 1 caught the ball, a point was won. If the ball did not make it over the roof, more attempts were made. I am not certain of all the details since it has been so long that we played it. Players today could make up some of their own original rules.

9. My younger brother, Alan, and I played softball in our yard by an apple tree. We hit the ball back and forth but did not run bases. There were times when we verbally disagreed loudly enough that the Amish neighbor man across the road whistled at us. I believe that was our cue to stop an argument.

10. A very simple game called "Button, Button, Whose Got the Button?" was played with our church friends as we sat on the porch steps with our eyes closed and our hands clasped. One player with eyes opened would place a button in someone's folded hands and say, "Button, button, whose got the button?" While we opened our eyes, we kept our hands folded as we guessed who received it. When the player was chosen correctly, that person would be next in charge.

11. My sister and I were fortunate to own a pair of roller skates that had to be attached to your shoes tightly and securely with a special roller skate key. Roller skating up and down our road gave us a lot of exercise and fun. Roller skate shoes were not available during our growing up years.

12. Two scooters provided a lot of fun as we rode them up and down our sidewalk. One was a red metal one in good condition and the other one was wooden that some people might have thrown in the trash. One leg remained on the main part

of the scooter while the other leg was used to propel it and gain momentum.

13. Homemade "walkie talkies" were improvised by attaching a long string onto each of the two opened tin cans. Talking and listening to the other person from a short distance provided some sound distortion but it was still possible to have reasonable communication.

14. Another simple listening and following direction game was "Simple Simon." If the person in charge would say, "Simple Simon says to wave your hand," all players should follow those directions without hesitation. However, if the directions omitted "Simple Simon says" and just exclaimed, "wave your hand," no players should follow that command. If so, they would be out of the game. Other simple commands might be: blink your eyes; stick out your tongue; touch your nose; stomp your foot; and smile.

15. Another simple game was "Tag." One person was "It" and tried to catch anyone running to tag them. If they were tagged, they were out of the game.

A CHALLENGE: HOMEMADE GAMES VERSUS TOYS FROM STORES

A challenge is to invite children to make up a game with their own rules or deviate in one or two ways with familiar ones to make some interesting changes. Perhaps we have lost something by furnishing children with toys from stores when there are many other delightful inexpensive games to be played. Two questions can be considered: What stimulates children the most when it comes to play activities? How can parents help to perpetuate imaginative and creative thinking in a society that is so gadget oriented?

Chapter 11
POTPOURRI OF MANY MEMORIES

Memories do not fade. They are very much a special part of our entire lives. Viewing our past as though it were through a kaleidoscope, what an assortment of events and changes have occurred that helped make us who we are today! Whether major or minor events, they all have affected us in some way.

The following potpourri of memories are in no particular order. Perhaps you can relate to many of these as you reflect on your own background and years of "growing up."

I had a Brownie camera that used black and white film with a flash attachment. The film was developed at a drug store. To make duplicate copies, it increased the cost. Most of these pictures were put in scrapbooks for student teachers and our family.

The wallpaper in the two living rooms was cleaned with a homemade cleaner that was doughy and spongy in nature. While standing on a ladder, a clump of the cleaner was rubbed over the wallpaper by hand to remove dust and smoke from the Glow Boy coal stove. It was not an easy job cleaning the ceiling for it was an "overuse" exercise for the arms and shoulders and a balancing stunt standing on a ladder!

Sending a USA first-class letter required a three-cent stamp. Compared with today, that was cheap. Now we can send emails and text people without a stamp. What a change!

Gas at the pump cost twenty-three cents a gallon. Compare that price today.

Our uncle who lived nearby had a sugar camp. After boiling the maple sap in the camp, some of it was brought to the house and reheated to a certain degree so that we could pull it like taffy! It was a strange sensation to feel the thick syrup harden in your fingers, and it was "finger-licking" good too!

The lawn was mowed with a reel or push mower. The blades would sometimes scoot over the grass and cut improperly if they needed sharpening or if the grass was a bit wet. The mower was then pushed backwards to make another attempt to mow that area again. We did not know what it would be like to have a self-propelled mower.

No fertilizer, insecticides, or pesticides were used on our lawn. There were different kinds of weeds that found easy spaces to grow. Mother encouraged me to take a knife and dig out the unwanted this-tles, buckcorns, plantains, and dandelions that were plentiful. (Mother commented once they had to **search** for dandelions when she was young). Digging weeds was a paying job as I was awarded a penny per thistle and a penny for twelve dandelions. While getting paid was an incentive, it was a miser's amount. I made sure I counted and recounted each weed to justify my pay. I enjoyed the digging, nevertheless, noting that those small spots looked cleaner and improved the appearance of the lawn.

S and H green stamps came in booklets published by the govern-ment. Some grocery commodities were rationed such as sugar and a required number of green stamps were taken from your booklet allowing you to purchase only a certain amount at one time. These stamps were given to the person at the cash register. Gas was another rationed product among other items.

Our nephew's young boys enjoyed digging our potatoes in the garden and found some that resembled an animal while stretching the imagination for others. The anticipation of what the next bunch of potatoes would resemble made the job more pleasurable.

Discipline was sitting on a chair for ten minutes with complete silence and nothing to do. My sister sat in one room and I sat in the kitchen. The distance between us was such that we could not see each other. The ten minutes seemed like an "eternity!" I remember it happening once.

An Amish neighbor built a thrashing machine and helped local farmers thrash their wheat that had been put into shocks. Neighbors helped each other with the thrashing. After the season ended, a big meal with ice cream was served when they all gathered for the last time.

Our Father liked sweets and bought a Baby Ruth candy bar that was at least a foot long. He bought orange slices for himself since he knew we did not like them very much. He also bought circus peanuts and Bonnie Doon ice cream which is still available.

Our rotary phone was hooked up to a party line system which was a nuisance. A neighbor might be using the phone and one could listen to the conversation as well as someone could listen to your phone chat. Sometimes a "long-winded" neighbor took advantage of the time by making you wait and wait until the phone line was free to make your call. Privacy did not seem to be an issue! At least there was an available phone to use in your own home. There were no cell phones, cordless phones or Wi-Fi, texting, sending and receiving emails, using the Internet, and other social media sources. They were unheard of.

Our family did not eat in restaurants or take advantage of drive-ins. We never questioned it, and I suppose our parents thought there was no need to eat at a restaurant when there was plenty of food at home. Another reason may have been that it was unwise to spend money on food and the accompanying service when not needed. The first time I had the opportunity to eat out, I was sixteen years old. I wondered at the time how one would know **how** and **what** to order. Eating in a restaurant was definitely a learning experience–so different from eating at home.

Terminology can change over the years. As a teacher teaching second grade pupils, our reading books were used primarily to teach children how to read and comprehend. Sometimes the stories expressed children being "happy" and "gay." Today the meaning of "gay" can have a different connotation. I remember hearing the phrase "that's cool" in reference to something being especially nice, and I realized in utter amazement that the meaning was used in a different context than what I was used to – weather conditions! Meals also changed by name. We always had dinner at noontime and supper in the evening. The word supper now seems obsolete. The word "dinner" is now the evening meal. Once we experienced such a mix-up and were wondering why our company did not show up for "dinner" (at noon time, of course!) Instead, they came in the evening for "dinner." We learned a mighty quick lesson in terminology.

Father built a garden fence with aluminum wires and white painted wooden fence posts that were cemented after being dug in the ground. The tops of the peaked posts were painted black. It made an attractive and sharp-looking fence around the garden. I had the long tedious job to paint each wire between the posts and occasionally repaint the posts and the peaks. However, there came a time when the fence was replaced with vinyl posts and a small garden gate that required no painting. What a relief that was!

Chickens were fed ground-up eggshells and mash in our chicken house. There were eggs to gather daily. The clucking hens liked to peck my hands as I reached under them to get their eggs. To prevent this, I thought of a "smart" idea. I got a board and held it against their beak while I reached quickly for their eggs, and I did not care whether they liked the board or not. Now they could go on their pecking spree using the board rather than my hands!

Among our batch of 100 chicks, there was a lame one. Mother named it Mephibosheth in reference to a crippled boy who was lame in both feet mentioned in II Samuel 4:4 of the Bible. Alan began to give it special attention and it became a pet that followed him around the yard. As he was lying down on the floor in the house one day, the chick crawled up his pant leg and tickled him intolerably. It was removed, of course. The little chick was kept in a cardboard box by the kitchen stove and became an unusual companion.

Watching my Father chop off a chicken's head and how it kept flopping around on the ground was not a pleasant sight. Cleaning our chickens after he was done with the "murder" was a chore I absolutely hated. It was the terrible stench or penetrating odor that could be smelled after the chicken was dunked very briefly in hot water so that the feathers could be pulled with more ease. I held my fingers on the left hand to pinch my nose because of the unbearable smell and pulled off the feathers with my right hand. I could not think of a more horrible job and there was no way to avoid it! How much easier it is to buy whole chickens or selected parts from a grocery store to prepare a good meal.

When Mother cooked chicken, I abhorred the skin unless it was fried to a crisp state. Once she made chicken patties for a meal. I took a bite and told her it tasted good which soon after I regretted my remark. I sensed there was chicken skin in those patties and asked her, "Do you have chicken skin in here?" She said, "Yes, I do!" From then on, not one more bite could be taken. I know Mother was unhappy, and I am sure she felt that I was very unreasonable. "Mind" can take over "matter" sometimes!

A large barrel of chicken mash was kept in our woodhouse. My sister and I chewed some of the mash as if it were chewing gum. Why did we eat it? I am not sure. I vaguely remember Mother telling us about how they chewed wheat kernels to make chewing gum. So we tried the mash and it worked too! We seldom had real gum to chew, but once in a while when we had bubble gum, we blew bubbles. I remember chewing gum and as I climbed into bed one night. The wad went on my bed post saving it for the next day! We did not think about germs!

Imagine heating three bedrooms upstairs with each room having a small register where a little heat could penetrate from the Glow Boy coal stove downstairs. Since it was not always comfortable to sleep upstairs in the winter, we used plenty of blankets and wore flannel pajamas. Hot water bottles were taken to bed to warm our feet. Later on, we used electric blankets that provided warmth and comfort. On very cold winter mornings, there might be frost inside the living room windows. A frosty area would be scratched with our fingers so we could look outside. Glow Boy was replaced with a floor furnace and later central heating with a hot water boiler system was installed. What a difference that made! Also, having hot water heat, Kinetico, and a humidity system has made our life much easier and better!

In the spring our upholstered furniture was cleaned with a wiry metal beater. No vacuum sweeper was purchased at our house at that time. With hardwood floors in the living rooms, a dry dust mop was used to collect the dust. Sometimes we were down on our hands and knees wiping the floors with a pail of water and a moist cloth. Finally, all the throw rugs were replaced with wall to wall carpeting in the two living rooms.

We had an old piece of equipment we called the corn sheller that shelled each ear of corn. When inserting the cob into a drop spot, cogs began to shell the corn while turning the handle. The cob went through a chute and landed in a basket. We raised our own corn to feed the chickens. Mother would take a corncob, stick it on a nail that was placed on a long stick, light a match, and hold it onto a limb of a tree that would kill hornets in a nest or worms embodied in silky looking webs. For many years there was still a bushel basket full of corncobs left after Mother died.

During my elementary years, I had a lot of sore throat and was absent from school from time to time. Mother knew her nutrition well and grated raw carrots for me with a hand grater. Then the carrots were squeezed with a cloth until there was juice. Her juicing helped me overcome my sore throat as I drank that every morning before I got on the bus and my body became healthier. What a dedicated hard-working Mother who was concerned about my health!

If I had sore throat, an antibiotic was usually not taken. Father had a bitter tasting "Boneset" tea to drink- almost not drinkable! An ointment was rubbed on my neck and a cloth wrapped around it to help alleviate the soreness. When I was a junior in high school, I contracted scarlet fever with a 104 temperature and a reddish skin color. With a raw feeling throat, Mother called the family doctor who came to the house – that was when doctors still made house calls. Mother surmised I had scarlet fever. When the doctor asked her what she thought I had, she said, "Scarlet fever." He told her that was correct. It was necessary for me to take an antibiotic. I was quarantined for two weeks and was absent from school during this time. Father's home remedy for scarlet fever was not appropriate in this case. Later on, at age twenty-four, I had a tonsillectomy – a major surgery for an adult!

When our sinuses were giving us a problem, the Indian chief Inhaler and Snuff, a yellow powder, were sniffed and inhaled through the nostrils even though there was a burning sensation. Going to the doctor for a sinus issue or taking an antibiotic was usually not done. Your own family "medicine cabinet" was used and no medical expenses occurred except for the products that had been purchased.

We never had the luxury of having good smelling powder or perfume. One day I visited one of our neighbor ladies who had such good smelling bottles on her dresser in her bedroom. As she went outdoors, I quickly went to her bedroom and snooped – opening lids or tops of containers on her dresser. I spilled the powder as I tried to hurry before she reentered the house. In fear, I ran home leaving the mess untouched and, unfortunately, left my coat and cap at her house. I ran into the house and told my Mother what had happened. I did not like her response as she said, "You have to go back and get your coat and cap and tell Ruth what you did." I thought I could not do that! Impossible! Face her? NO! But I knew I had to go back and make a confession. I was so nervous as I told her the truth. She was kind to me, and I do not remember a scolding from her. That was one of the most difficult lessons of my life and I never forgot it!

Cattails are wetland plants with flowering spikes and flat blade-like leaves that grow to be three to ten feet tall. The top portion has a seedy brown head fluff when it is ripe. They often grow along ditches. My Mother told us how to color their heads by cutting the stem before the head gets too ripe or brown because the inside can burst and then the spike is spoiled. After the brown is scraped gently with a knife, crayons are used to color the spike. One solid color or several colors can be used to make stripes. After they are colored, they should be allowed to dry. The spikes can then be twisted gently to make another kind of design. Cattails make intriguing bouquets. I took a bouquet to my classroom and we also sold them. It is a unique work of art!

Company might come to your house without any advanced notice. There was no need for them to call us or for us to call them if we wanted to visit. You just dropped by! Getting unexpected visitors was a common occurrence. Taking time to visit and inviting them to come back again was part of the "normal" social life. Are we missing something today?

Some years ago, one of our neighbors wanted a building moved to another location on their property. No equipment was used as many strong-muscled men stood all around the four sides of the building and lifted it at the count of 1-2-3. It was an astonishing feat to see it happen. It was certainly a cooperative demonstration of man-power!

Mother was like a nutritionist and read widely about preventing disease and staying healthy. Raw sunflower seeds were ground in an old coffee grinder which we still have on our buffet today. Mother's stepmother had a 40+ year old parrot and it was so healthy. It was fed sunflower seeds daily, so Mother believed that if they are healthy for a parrot, they must be good for her too. My sister and I continue to eat **raw** sunflower seeds daily also.

Christmas at our house was not a time for a lot of festivities. We hung our socks up one evening and by morning, our humorous Father had filled them with corncobs! Much later in life, we exchanged names, bought gifts, and shared them at our family Christmas get-together. The Christmas story was sometimes read for the younger children to enjoy. Finally, we reached the point where we contributed money to a charity rather than exchanging gifts.

Late in the summer there were flickering yellow lights flying through our yard when it was dark. We called them lightning bugs; others called them fireflies. We would try to catch them, pinch off the lighting part of their body, and then hold it under our nose. Literature states that only the females flicker their lights to attract the males.

Ice cream was a specialty at our house. When we knew our parents were planning a trip to the grocery store, we would beg (ask) them to bring home ice cream. Once Father, my younger brother, Alan, and I ate a gallon of ice cream while sitting at the table enjoying every bite! Fortunately, none of us got sick. If homemade ice cream was made, licking the dasher was a special treat.

We have attended special Pennsylvania Dutch gatherings arranged by those that speak the language. A meal is served and a special program is provided with congregational singing. Of course, mostly Mennonites and Amish attend. We were told should someone hear us speak English, we would be fined a dollar. They were fun gatherings.

Computers did not exist when I was growing up, so we typed on manual typewriters and later on electric ones. Our fingers exerted a lot of pressure on those keys. To return the carriage, it was slung back and forth by hand manually. Ribbons required changing when the print became too dim to read. It was best not to make mistakes but when they were made, there were special pencils with erasers to remove the errors. There were also bottles with a white liquid and a brush that could be rubbed over the errors. The correct word or spelling could then be retyped over it leaving a fainter copy.

Typing accurately was of great importance when preparing multiple copies of a page that was typed on a sheet with carbon paper attached behind it. When a typing error needed correction, sometimes I used a razor blade or brushed liquid "white out" over it. The sheet was removed from the carbon and placed in the zerox or mimeograph machine that was turned by hand. Now the task is so much simpler with access of printers and copiers that can make multiple copies in a hurry without using carbon paper.

I am not aware that we heard news on terrorism, riots, or insurrections. Those words did not exist in our vocabulary. We felt quite secure at home even without locking our doors at night. People seemed more "sane and courteous!"

We grew up without television or radio. Some media channels today include Facebook, Twitter, Instagram, and the Internet. Other communicative devices are iPhones, e-readers, tablets, and Smart phones. They can be purchased easily. We can add texting and sending emails too. Can these gadgets ever replace a human voice that needs to be heard sometimes? Are we losing our connectedness or is it still there but in a different form? Technical devices have changed a lot of things in our lives. Years ago, we used only phones, wrote letters, or visited people sometimes unannounced. The pace of living was slower. Everything has now become faster but does it cause more stress?

Hickory nuts and black walnuts were cracked on a flat piece of iron with a forceful pounding of the hammer and sometimes pieces flying in all directions in the kitchen. What a job it was to dig out the meat with a nutpick from the cracked shells. We had neighbor children who stole some of our walnuts from the tree near the road but eventually they got caught. I told them this was private property and permission was necessary to take them. I visited their parents and the stealing stopped. One child returned with money and one with apples for recompense. I told them what really mattered was their change of behavior.

Packages purchased in stores were often wrapped in rolls of paper that was torn or cut off at the appropriate place. String was then tied to the package. Mother would save string and roll it into a ball. Wrapping paper was also saved if it was not torn or wrinkled too much.

Library paste was purchased in a jar. Now we have Elmer's Glue and Goo Gone. Glue bottles with rubber-like tips were used in school. The bottle and the fingers would quickly become a sticky mess!

Our parents were not fashion-interested people. There was no need to "keep up with the neighbors" or have many of the modern conveniences and appliances that people felt were so necessary. The mother usually stayed at home to take care of the children, perform household duties, and make the meals. The father was considered the "breadwinner." In some situations, today it takes both parents working to make ends meet. Getting baby sitters, sending children to pre-school and Day Care Centers, or to their grandparents have helped. How did our parents function years ago without all this extra help? How many homes today have one parent that stays home with the younger children?

Some women's hosiery in certain stores could be found inside egg-shaped containers. They were usually more expensive and available in a variety of colors.

While we were in the elementary grades, we wore underwear. The lower back had flaps that we called "barn doors." The bottom of the legs often got stretched and became too big to fit well, so the bottom cuff was rolled over the ankles underneath our stockings making a bulge. Of course, we had to be mindful that the stocking seam ran straight down the back of the leg.

Smith Brothers' black licorice cough drops came in a box and tasted good enough to suck on like candy whether you had a cough or not.

When some men's pants material seemed so limp and needed stiffening, starch was added to the water and then a pants stretcher was used to dry them. White shirt collars were also starched.

Early school desks had lids that raised up and down. Each desk had an ink well to place a bottle of ink. The pens were then dipped into the bottle before writing. Years ago, people who used these ink pens had quite a flair when writing in cursive. They wrote elaborately and beautifully. Now we use markers, ball point pens, and other kinds of efficient writing tools.

My sister and I often went bike riding on country roads with our three-speed blue and red Schwin bikes on a Sunday afternoon. One afternoon while we were biking south on our way home, a car from the east on State Road 6 turned onto our road. The unfamiliar gentleman stopped and said, "You're just the girls I've been looking for!" I understood clearly what he had said but I responded with a terse, "What?" I glanced quickly at his license plate and saw the two-number prefix which placed him in Nobles Country southeast of our county. We pedaled as fast as we could for fear he would turn around and follow us. We crossed State Road 6 and then took the country road we lived on knowing there would be a good number of houses we could stop by if necessary. Fortunately, he did not follow us. I do not know when our three-speed bikes went so fast. Until we got home, we were perspiring and our faces were red hot! Home never looked so good!

Mother never wasted food and sometimes the mixture looked like "who knows what!" Left-overs were a common meal and often some bread would be broken in pieces to add quantity. Father would say occasionally, "What 'bomzooligan' is this?" His made-up term and the tone of his voice indicated some skepticism of whether to eat it. Today we can buy lots of "bomzooligan" in grocery stores, especially at the Deli.

Meat was purchased and ground into hamburger at home. The cracklings were a delicacy for us since we seldom had them.

Every day we biked to one of our neighbors to get a gallon of raw milk that was always cooled in cold water in one of their buildings. Occasionally we had home-made butter. Now drinking raw milk is considered unsafe as we are told milk needs to be pasteurized or homogenized. If there were any infectious diseases, we survived them all while drinking raw milk.

There were two outside pumps or wells. One was a cistern with soft rain water and the other was drinking water or hard water. Today, inspectors tell us that water would not be safe to drink. The well is not deep enough! However, we are still very much alive today!

Unwanted tramps stopped by occasionally and got water from our well by the west porch. We once invited a tramp to eat with us at the kitchen table. His one hand always remained in his pocket for unknown reasons to us, and he never spoke a word while sitting at the table. He seemed to appreciate the meal. He had chocolate pie smeared on his face. He rubbed his stomach and patted his head at the same time to show us in his own way that he appreciated the food. It was an unverbalized "thank you." None of us felt at ease with him, and we will never know more about his weird or strange behavior. It was an uncomfortable experience!

One other time we fed a tramp that dumped some of his food over our chicken fence. They benefited from his apparent ungratefulness. We wondered why he did that!

Cats have always been important members of our family. Usually, our cats were strays and not taken to a veterinarian. One cat, Tuffy. had become ill with cat distemper and formed a sore on the front of his head. My sister reasoned that if the Indian Chief Inhaler helped my Father's sinuses, it might help this sick cat. Gently she held the inhaler to his nose and persisted with this treatment for a number of days. To our surprise, the cat survived. Maybe the herbal ingredients helped him! The cats we have had for the last while have been taken to the vet. Our last cat, Rocky, who was a stray and stayed with us for fourteen years, was put to sleep the early part of December 2019. He was such a part of our family and we miss him dearly. We bought a little marker and buried him by our garden fence not far from the flowers and bird feeders.

HOW IT USED TO BE

Assessing the activities, events, and circumstances of our younger years which seems like long ago, there were many challenges, adjustments, and issues to face that, hopefully, have made us stronger psychologically and spiritually today.

Three vital questions may be asked: Do our modern and current ways of life bring us more happiness, trust, contentment, and faith in God and humanity? Do they give us more time to build precious family relationships and our circle of friends? What really matters in life?

How can we share our valuable past history with our families, our children, grandchildren, and generations to come?

BIBLICAL ADMONITIONS

Several verses should be an encouragement to all of us:
- *Acts 20:21- "...turn to God in repentance and have faith in our Lord Jesus Christ."*

- *Hebrews 4:16 – "Let us then approach the throne of grace with confidence so that we may receive mercy and find grace to help us in our time of need."*
- *Psalms 100:5 – "For the Lord is good and his love endures forever; his faithfulness continues through all generations."*

ACROSTIC REMINISCENT OF THE HOCHSTETLER FAMILY

Thoroughly enjoyed reading
Hard working parents
Enjoyed singing together

Humorous father
Occasionally went shopping
Creative mother
Helped others
Stamp collector brother
Travelers to different countries
Entertained grandchildren
Talked Pennsylvania Dutch and English
Lived with Christian principles
Enjoyed having company
Raised five children

Fun playing games
Accomplished a lot of work
Musical father
Idleness was not evident
Lived a frugal life
Yearly washed and waxed car

CPSIA information can be obtained
at www.ICGtesting.com
Printed in the USA
BVHW040009250821
614913BV00005B/20